HAND
IN
HAND

A TRUE STORY BY JANE COUPES

~

This is a true and honest account of my experiences of coping as a family with my husband, Dominic, and our two small children, after enduring a stroke approximately ten days after the birth of my son.

Illustrated by John Philbin
Edited by Gill Todd
Cover Design by Dominic Coupes
Photography by Michelle Wilde
Physiotherapy information by Tina Betts

Printed in Victoria, BC, Canada.

ISBN: 978-1-4251-8509-1 (Soft)

 www.trafford.com

North America & international
toll-free: 1 888 232 4444 (USA & Canada)
phone: 250 383 6864 ♦ fax: 812 355 4082 ♦ email: info@trafford.com

For Dominic, Emily and Daniel -
my driving force and reasons to get out of bed in the morning.

Preface

The idea for this book came about shortly after arriving home after spending six long and gruelling months in a rehabilitation hospital. Despite having two very young children, one of whom was my newborn son, my husband and our two families had coped extremely well, rallying around in that Irish Catholic way, so even though I was away from home every job had been covered by another family member. Although I would not have chosen for it to be any different, in the days following my discharge, I felt as though I did not have a role any more, despite being a survivor and still having to continue my rehabilitation to achieve the best recovery possible. I was too frail to leave the house without being accompanied, so needed some direction.

Technically on maternity leave, but still undergoing a massive rehabilitation, I was therefore subjected to daytime television, and watched lots of real-life accounts of people who had overcome adverse medical conditions. I watched one such programme and thought, I should write my story. My boss had always told me that I wrote excellent business letters, but I also felt compelled to tell my story in case I could in anyway help another young stroke survivor.

Although the book has taken just over four years to write, there were long periods during that time when I put it on hold, as I felt there were more important and time-critical issues to deal with, i.e. developing and nurturing my relationship with my son, pursuing my physical recovery, sorting out my crazy mixed-up head, moving house to a new area and getting life back to some sort of normality.

Why should you read my story over any other? Well, I feel it is an inspirational story, with a different angle involving the children, an extraordinary family, friendship and I guess also a love story.

Contents

Introduction

The woman lay completely flat on the hospital bed. There was no pillow. She was totally paralysed. Her hair was shoulder length back then and instead of being strewn all over her pale drawn face in a tragic way as you may imagine, her relatives thought it was disturbingly neat. She was on a bed on the high-dependency unit after suffering a massive stroke that morning, although she herself was still unaware of this. Her relatives did not know if she would survive the night. The medical team ran to and from her bedside; it was a life threatening emergency situation and the woman was indeed fighting for her life!

The experienced cardiology consultant went home late that evening utterly baffled, and thought about his young patient. She had already been a patient on the high-dependency unit for a few days with a rare heart condition called post-partum cardiomyopathy, which in itself can have a 50 per cent mortality rate. The woman had delivered a baby boy ten days before, but what could possibly have caused her to have a major stroke and for her heart to be in such a critical condition?

That woman was me.

This is my story...

PART ONE:

EMERGENCY

The Shortest
Time at Home

On returning home with baby, Daniel, on the day he was born, things were initially fine, but that was all to change soon. Thus, to the immediate and dramatic events that forced me to be horizontal on that bed in the HDU...

Drifting in and out of consciousness, slumped over four sofa cushions piled high whilst sitting on the sofa in our lounge for the entire night, was categorically the most unpleasant and horrific experience, and one that I shall never forget throughout the course of time. I was approximately five days post-partum and this was the point when my health took a turn for the worse and it was also when the funny breathing started.

My body started making a peculiar sound when I attempted to lie down at night. This prevented me from sleeping soundly. I can only describe it as a hissing, gurgling noise in my chest. It reminded me of the noise of the gas and air in the delivery suite when I had been stitched and, after having vivid flashbacks to that time, I mentioned this to my husband, Dom. In the end I could not even lean back in an upright chair without it happening. Dom and I had lots of sleepless nights, with him telling me to lie back and do my best to ignore it and me protesting that I just couldn't.

The funny thing was that on some of those sleepless nights, our son, Daniel, had actually started sleeping almost through the night, so in the day he was full of beans and we were completely shattered! This weird breathing was making me feel quite stressed, as if I had palpitations. This went on for about five nights, and I became paler and weaker until one afternoon when Daniel was due for a feed, I was just so exhausted and weak that Dom had to hold our son to my breast while he suckled. Strangely, when he was feeding, I felt calmer and the hissing noise seemed to ease.

That night I could not sleep or even lie down in bed again. I ended up sitting downstairs all night in our lounge with four sofa cushions on my lap and my head resting on top of them. I stayed like that all night long, with the television on in the background tuned to the VH1 music channel. I had no sleep whatsoever, although I can remember having a strange sensation as though I was floating or drowning. I call it my Nirvana moment, although it certainly didn't feel like paradise to me! Nearly all of my generation will remember the iconic album cover, *Never Mind*, with the baby floating in water, swimming towards the dollar bill, and my predicament completely reminded me of it, except I was not submerged in water, instead I was drowning in my own body fluid!

Below I have included Dominic's succinct version of the short time that we had at home together as a family.

JANE COUPES

Saturday, 24th February, 2001.

Jane gave birth to a baby boy (Daniel) at around 9 a.m. in the morning. The birth was relatively quick, having taken approximately three hours from the onset of labour to giving birth. Mother and baby went home at around 7 p.m. the same day. Jane began breastfeeding Daniel. We already had a 22-month-old little girl, Emily.

Sunday, 25th February, 2001 to Thursday, 1st March.

Daily visits from the midwives. Jane had slight swelling of the ankles and baby was jaundiced. Jane was told that neither condition was anything to be concerned about.

Practice doctor visited on 26th February, but did not examine Jane.

Friday, 2nd March, 2001.

Jane started to complain about having a sore throat and asked me to buy her some cough medicine (Benylin). Another visit from the midwife.

Saturday, 3rd March, 2001.

Jane didn't have a very good night's sleep and was complaining that she felt strangely anxious and had palpitations. A different midwife came and suggested that it was probably just the after-effects of the birth and maybe a touch of post-natal depression.

Sunday, 4th March, 2001.

Again, Jane had a very bad night's sleep (probably about four hours in total). She said that she felt extremely anxious and that her pulse seemed to be racing. She got upset, so I decided to see if the midwife would come and visit (it had been agreed that no one would come that day). The midwife listened to what Jane had to say and again it was suggested that it was something post-natal.

Monday, 5th March, 2001.

Jane had an even worse night and wasn't able to sleep at all. She said that she was unable to lie down, as when she did, she felt/heard a gurgling sound in her throat that reminded her of the gas and air when she was giving birth. She was extremely tired and still complained that she was anxious and that her pulse was racing. I decided to ring the midwife and ask if she could call the doctor to take a look at Jane. The doctor arrived at around lunchtime and listened to what Jane had to say. As well as the anxiety, gurgling and racing pulse, Jane also explained about her slightly swollen ankles and her sore throat. In addition we asked about baby's jaundice and his sticky eyes.

Without examining her (apart from looking down her throat, for say, five seconds) he suggested that it was some sort of post-natal anxiety and prescribed one month's supply of beta blockers, which were supposed to calm her down (Propanalol 40mg - one three times a day). In addition, he prescribed Nystan Pastilles (one four times a day) for her throat. Immediately, I went to the chemist and returned to allow Jane time to take one Propanalol 40mg tablet at around 3 p.m. and another at around 10 p.m. That night Jane seemed to get worse. She complained that she couldn't even lean back, as when she did she felt/heard the gurgling sound in her throat. I asked her to show me what she meant and the noise I heard was like the sound of a kettle boiling inside her throat/chest.

Meanwhile, Jane was breastfeeding every three to four hours and she was becoming weaker and weaker to the point where at 3 a.m. on Monday night/Tuesday morning, I had to hold the baby onto her. She had not had any sleep for around 48-60 hours. Between

5 a.m. and 6 a.m. I decided to call the emergency doctor. The doctor came, examined Jane and admitted her immediately by ambulance to Stepping Hill Hospital, Stockport.

Jane was admitted back onto the delivery suite of the maternity unit. She had massive amounts of fluid on her lungs and was put on oxygen. Her heart rate was around 130bpm. Jane was examined by a number of doctors, the last of whom explained that there appeared to be a problem with her heart. It wasn't functioning properly and this had caused blood to back up on her lungs. She was subsequently moved to the HDU.

Jane had a number of tests including an ultrasound 'echo' scan. Later in the evening, the heart consultant came and explained to us that Jane had a condition called post-partum cardiomyopathy and that she should expect to stay in hospital for around six weeks.

Wednesday, 7th March, 2001.

Jane was relatively comfortable on HDU, although her heart rate was around 130bpm. She had been started on a whole array of drugs mostly administered intravenously.

Thursday, 8th March, 2001.

Unfortunately, at around 10 a.m. the next morning, Jane suffered a major stroke affecting around one third of the right side of her brain. She was transferred to the coronary care unit and she remained there for ten days.

Friday, 9th March to Sunday, 18th March, 2001.

In CCU, Jane was unable to eat for herself for a couple of days, but slowly came around. She was unable to move her left arm or leg, and the left side of her face was also affected.

Monday, 19th March to Sunday, 1st April, 2001.
Jane was transferred from CCU to Ward A11 at Stepping Hill Hospital and stayed there for two weeks.

Monday, 2nd April, 2001.
Jane was transferred from Ward A11 at Stepping Hill Hospital to the Devonshire Centre for Neuro Rehabilitation, also in Stockport, and stayed there for six months, coming home most weekends.

Friday, 28th September, 2001.
Jane was discharged from The Devonshire.

Our versions of events are practically the same, except I have tried to give more detail.

Dominic took the first week after Daniel was born as paternity leave. On the Monday he told me that he was going to run a few errands, including registering Daniel's birth, and would return later that afternoon.

Even as a second time mum and technically an expert, I was a little worried how I would cope with the two children by myself; however, after he had left I began my daily routine of preparing breakfast for myself and the children, putting a washer load on and trying to generally tidy the house a little. Daniel was strapped in his car seat, but safely in the middle of the kitchen table, and while Emily and I were finishing off our breakfast, the sound of the washing machine lulled him into a nice deep sleep. I now only had to deal with Emily for a few hours while Daniel had a good sleep.

I can remember feeling a little fraught around lunchtime, as Daniel was awake now and Emily was becoming more demanding. Just then the doorbell rang and it was my new GP from the practice around the corner from our new house, to do my post-natal check. He came in for five minutes, asked how things were going and then left. When I closed the door, I felt relieved that he had gone so quickly, as it had been a bad time to call, and I could now sort out the children's lunch. However, I also made a mental note of how markedly different this check had been than when we lived at the old house in Marple, and I had had Emily. That time it had been a female doctor who had called at a pre-arranged time. She had come inside, asked me lots of relevant questions, given me a thorough examination, given Emily a thorough examination and checked that I was booked in for a smear test soon.

My nights without any sleep because of the hissing noise continued and during the days I spoke to most of the midwives on the local team, who said that I could be suffering from post-natal depression or post-traumatic stress disorder, as the birth had been so quick - three hours from the first contraction to Daniel's head coming out! They advised me to have a relaxing warm bath or a glass of wine to try and chill out. In the meantime, as well as the funny breathing I had developed a very scratchy sore throat. The midwife arranged for the new GP to call again and he examined my throat, prescribed some lozenges and said that I probably had a touch of depression. He then also prescribed some beta blockers to try and stop the palpitations, and left.

By this time I started to feel that something was clearly wrong. My mum and dad, Dom and his mum and dad had become increasingly worried until that night after I had taken two of the tablets, I had another sofa night with the drowning sensation, only this time it was much worse.

Very early the next morning Dom rang the doctors co-operative in our area and asked for someone to come out and examine me. As we waited for the doctor, I asked Dom to kneel down and listen to the funny breathing sound in my chest, and he said that I sounded like a kettle boiling! He also said that my lips had gone blue (I later found out that I had been in a collapsed state because I was in heart failure).

The doctor arrived. He was a very smart mature man and I immediately felt that he would diagnose my problem. He examined my ankles and legs, and listened intently to Dom, who told him what had been happening. He then listened to my chest through a stethoscope and immediately started to look very concerned. He said he had to go outside and make a phone call and he would be back soon to let us know what was happening.

He came back inside and said that there was a problem with my lungs and that he had telephoned an ambulance, which was on the way. I asked him if I had time to nip to the loo and he said there was no time!

Next thing the blue light ambulance came into the close. I was wearing my pyjamas, slippers and dressing gown, and two paramedics bundled me into a wheelchair, wrapped me in a blanket, tipped me back, lifted me into the ambulance and turned on the siren. Dom said he would meet me at the hospital with Daniel and he went to drop Emily off with my mum and dad, who lived nearby.

～

I arrived back at the maternity section of the hospital and was taken back up to a delivery suite. In the room there was a team of doctors who immediately went to work, quickly and efficiently trying to find out what was wrong with me. Although I was terrified, they were extremely professional and made me feel very at ease and content that they would do everything possible to make me comfortable. The paramedics had already given me an oxygen mask to wear in the ambulance and I immediately started to feel better. Two of the young doctors dressed in green scrubs seemed particularly intent on diagnosing what was the matter with me, one was female and the other was a young male with twinkling eyes! They did numerous blood tests, gave me some different oxygen, arranged X-rays, gave me several injections and inserted a catheter as a formality - the complete works!

After a long period of investigation, they came back to me and said that my lungs were full of fluid. This was a bi-product of the fact that my heart was not working properly. They said that I would have to see a heart consultant, Dr Lewis, later that day. Meanwhile, they would have to administer some serious drugs, and the bed manager would try and arrange a bed where Daniel could stay with me.

A while later he came back and said there was a bed on the high-dependency unit and there was a small side room where I could keep Daniel with me. These plans were soon changed when they realised that it was not advisable for me to breastfeed Daniel any more when I had such serious drugs in my bloodstream, which were being given intravenously. I also had so many tubes and wires attached to me that I could not have got Daniel's mouth anywhere near my nipple!

This time all passed in a whirl and a complete daze, and later I struggled to comprehend that I had only spent ten days at home and now I was back in hospital again, this time as what felt like a prisoner!

~

Daniel is my second child and I had already sailed through one pregnancy and birth, so I thought I would give you a little more information about the build-up to Daniel's birth. The chapter 'A Bundle of Pink' covers the details of my first pregnancy for comparison, without any hiccups or life-threatening events!

My daughter, Emily, experienced all her first events whilst we were living on Kayswood Road in Marple; first crawl, always backwards at first until she had backed herself under the coffee table, her first steps, first tooth, first holiday to Oasis along with Dom's parents when our journey began from Marple. Her christening was when she was 11 months and the ceremony was at Holy Spirit Church in Marple. Afterwards we had a meal at Almonds restaurant, and our immediate family and friends came back to Kayswood Road for drinks and to watch Emily open her christening gifts.

When Emily had just turned one, Dominic and I noticed some new houses being built in Offerton on the way to my mum and dad's house. The new site was called St John's Wood and was being built on by both Barratt Homes and Bellway Homes. After looking around the show houses, we decided to part exchange our house in Marple and to buy one of the brand new bigger houses, and this also prompted us to start thinking about expanding our family.

We were aware that another addition would change our lives completely, even more so than when we had had Emily almost two years previously. We had all the usual hopes and aspirations that come with buying a new house and having a larger family. We faced the prospect of extra work with trepidation. We could never have imagined how this normal life-changing event would dramatically alter our lives temporarily beyond belief.

I remember picking Mum up lots of times on the way to the new building site, and she then looked after Emily while I was busy deciding which kitchen cupboards, bathroom tiles etc., I wanted in our new property. On moving day I will always remember that Emily fell from the top of the stairs at Kayswood Road to the very bottom. I watched my daughter topple down the stairs like a little floppy rag doll and it seemed to happen in slow-motion until I saw she was all right then I stopped hyperventilating.

Looking back, we discovered that Daniel had been conceived on that very first weekend in the new house. My pregnancy was very similar to the first time with Emily and we were both convinced that we were having another little girl. The only difference this time was that I seemed to be more tired, but I had expected this because now I already had a toddler running around the house needing lots of attention.

As the weeks went by my bump grew. It became a neat little bump and strangers could not even tell that I was with child. One day I was going to work as usual when I suddenly felt very sick and disorientated. I had to keep getting on and off the train to get some air. I eventually got to Manchester Piccadilly Station and, after a short rest on a nearby bench, I walked the short distance to my place of work. When I got there, my friend, Cath, asked me what was the matter and she said that I looked as white as a sheet. She gave me her mobile phone number and told me that if the dizziness ever happened again while I was pregnant, she would come up to the station and escort me to the office. She sat me down, gave me some water and went to the shop to get some biscuits to raise my sugar levels. I was very concerned for my own welfare and worried that I would lose my baby.

After this initial hiccup, my pregnancy seemed to continue at a normal pace. The midwives told me that the baby was a little on the small side, and closely monitored the situation with regular scans. The weeks went by and eventually it was a couple of weeks before my due date.

The evening before I had the baby, Dominic and I went out for a meal with my brother, my cousin and their wives. This was a regular event that we tried to do every couple of months without taking the children. This time Andrew and Paul had won in choosing the venue, so we ended up in an Indian restaurant in Hazel Grove. All the usual jokes came out about a curry bringing about the onset of labour, and we sat and had a lovely meal together, with nice food and lots of laughs! I joked about having twinges during the meal, but really they were just Braxton Hicks. Dom used to joke and say:

"Toni Braxton is in the house!"

This outing was a bit like history repeating itself, as when I had Emily we had been out a few evenings before my due date with some friends, Tony and Lucy. That time it had been just out for a few drinks (lemonade for me!) in Gee Cross, near Hyde, and I remember writing in Emily's baby book that Daddy had been out the night before she was born and had drank several pints of Carling Premier!

I awoke early the next morning and started to have contractions. Very soon they became very close together and quite violent. I told Dom to ring my mum and dad, and put them on standby to come and get Emily while we went to the hospital, and then I went into the shower. Dom helped me to dry myself off when I came out. "You had better ring my dad back and tell them to come over right now!" I said.

My contractions had become so strong that my whole body was shaking and I felt like some natural force had taken over my body. It had been like this with Emily, but the midwife had warned me that your second baby is always quicker.

"Let's go to the hospital and get us another baby," said Dom.

My midwife had already suggested to me that if I was to have another child, I should consider a home birth because there might not be enough time to get to hospital.

When Mum and Dad arrived, I somehow managed to get into our car and Dom drove to the hospital. While I was booking in a midwife came downstairs to the reception area. She looked at my face, now screwed up in pain, wheeled me in a chair straight to the delivery suite and shouted to her colleague.

"We're in business here!"

Again the birth was straightforward, but very quick, and I can remember feeling shocked and a tiny little bit disappointed when they said I had delivered a baby boy. This feeling soon went away when I breastfed him and I started to think that it would be nice for Dom to have a son to do the football thing with and also we now had one of each sex - the perfect family! Before we had Daniel, we had said that deep down we both wanted another little girl, really for Emily to play with, and also because at that time all our friends and family who had little boys said they were hard work and very boisterous.

This time with Daniel, I was adamant that I was not going to stay overnight in hospital. This was quite a normal thing to do after a subsequent child. Dominic came back at lunchtime, after making all the phone calls to tell family and friends the joyful news and getting a few last minute things from Mothercare. He brought me a lovely, big, fresh, ham salad sandwich and a huge bag of my favourite spring onion crisps from Marks & Spencer. I can remember eating them and looking around at the other ladies in the small ward, and feeling sorry for them because they had sad tired NHS sandwiches. As soon as lunch was over, I asked Dom to go and find out when we could take Daniel home. I had to hang around a while to wait for a doctor to check Daniel out, but we eventually went home during the early evening at about 7 p.m.

When we got home, Matthew, my neighbour's eldest son, was out playing football in the close. He ran to their front door shouting.

"Jane's already home with the baby!"

This struck me as being strange at the time because then he was probably age seven or eight and I can remember thinking that it was nice of him to show so much interest when boys of that age were not usually the slightest bit interested in babies. Anyway, they all came outside, checked Daniel out and said how gorgeous he was.

After that we soon slipped back into the pattern of sleepless nights, nappies and what seemed like always having to stay in because we were expecting the midwife to call.

I expressed concern to my midwife that my ankles were very swollen. They had swelled up after Emily's birth, but had gone down again a few days later back to the nice slim ankles of which I had been particularly proud. This time they did not seem to be going down and I told Dom I had fat old ladies' ankles!

I can vividly remember one time when Daniel awoke in the night for a feed that I was excessively over-tired and I ended up losing my temper.

"Peter, please stop crying and go back to sleep," I said.

I was so disorientated; I had called my own son the wrong name!

Now I could not climb the stairs without becoming breathless, and as the days went by I became paler and weaker, and I quickly lost all my weight from the pregnancy again as I had with Emily. This was all familiar territory, so I expressed my concerns to my midwife, but was not really too alarmed myself. That is until the peculiar breathing started.

Emergency Care

I got settled on the HDU and Dominic and I made an executive decision that it was not wise to keep Daniel with me. This was not only because of the reasons I have already mentioned, but I was just so poorly that I could not have coped with a new baby. Dom said he would take Daniel home and look after both Daniel and Emily if he could arrange some compassionate leave from work.

This then gave us the problem of how Dominic would feed Daniel. I had planned to breastfeed him for at least six months, as I had with Emily. I knew Dom was a bit of a hero to take them both on, but even he could not perform miracles! Now breastfeeding was no longer feasible, the nurses contacted the maternity ward and gave Dom two boxes of ready prepared bottles, which they usually gave to new mums who were bottle-feeding.

As a mum I had wanted to treat my children the same where possible. Having to stop breastfeeding Daniel early made me feel that I had given him a raw deal already. Later this issue was to become a recurring theme.

JANE COUPES

During this investigative time, I also had to have an echocardiogram, and dozens of ECG tests. The 'echo' scan is an ultrasound of your heart and I was completely transfixed, as on the screen I could see the usual black cone shape of the area being scanned and then within that I could see my heart and even the valves flapping. Intermittently the screen was changed and I could see a series of colours flashing across the screen, which indicated the blood flow through my heart. It was fascinating to me, but I was also deeply concerned as the sonographer seemed to be doing a really thorough check and didn't say a single word throughout the examination. A lot later on, I learned that practically the whole of the cardiology team had stood around late that night watching video footage of my heart scan and wondering what could possibly have happened to someone my age to make my heart so enlarged and to be pumping so slowly.

That afternoon Dominic came back to the hospital with the children and said that work had been fine and he would take time off to raise our family in the near future. When we both met Dr Lewis later, he explained that I had a condition called post-partum cardiomyopathy and I could expect to be in hospital for at least six weeks, possibly longer! At the time the thought of spending six weeks in hospital was horrendous. Had I known the eventual outcome, I would have found six weeks easy. At least I was more comfortable now and my breathing had eased slightly.

As I settled in my bed on the HDU, it was immediately obvious where, thankfully, a large portion of the money in the NHS goes. The entire back wall was full of high-tech equipment, some of which I was rigged up to.

I immediately took a shine to Dr Lewis. He was like a mad professor; very charismatic, with a gentle and caring nature.

He always looked immaculate and wore his trademark bow tie with his pinstriped suit. He lifted his arms up above his head and almost hung onto the overhead curtain rails that go around the beds. He looked like a monkey while he told Dom, myself and his team/audience of medics in detail about my condition.

He later told me that one of his daughters had just delivered a baby boy, so he kind of related to me and Daniel as well. He explained that post-partum cardiomyopathy is a condition that is more prevalent in Third World countries and it only happens in the Western World in something like one in every 30,000 pregnancies. It had happened to me probably because I had been diagnosed with Crohn's disease when I was seventeen.

Crohn's disease is a problem that occurs in the intestines (in my case exactly where the small and large intestine join together). Although Crohn's can be a chronic illness alone, I had managed to live a practically normal life and have a relatively successful career, as we had managed to keep it under control with regular medication. I can still remember times when I had been managing my team at work one minute and then the next I was bent double with the pain in my tummy and sent home by my boss. I thought this was an instrumental factor in both my successful and very quick labours, as I already had a fairly high pain barrier! However, because I already had an absorption problem with the vitamins and minerals from my diet, I was already prone to feeling very tired a lot of the time and very occasionally had a problem with abdominal bleeding.

So, back to my second pregnancy... Even though I had been eating a healthy diet throughout, my stomach had not properly digested and absorbed the nutrients from the food, so, coupled with the fact that any baby takes a lot of the mother's nutrients by the very nature of its growth, consequently, I was technically malnourished and, therefore, more susceptible to heart problems.

The details that follow during my hospital stay are how I remember them, but I was so poorly they may be a bit sketchy, only in terms of the order that things happened. I was closely monitored by the doctors and nurses, and I set myself the task of remembering all their names. This was probably partly to do with my old job, which was working part-time in human resources for Barclays Bank. I knew this was good for building relationships, and also at the time there was nothing better to do!

I soon settled into a hospital routine on the HDU and quickly adjusted to the fact that I was now wired up to all this equipment, and I only had to move fractionally and alarms sounded next to my bed. My heart monitor had been set to alarm if my heart rate climbed above a certain figure. I can remember trying to keep still, but feeling very shocked when all I did was clean my teeth and my heart rate went through the roof, right up to 130bpm. On reflection, I joked and blamed this on my dad, who had always been in the bathroom with me when I was a little girl and we were getting ready for school and work. He has always cleaned his teeth vigorously and now, without realising it, I was doing the same, but this time it was detrimental to my health.

One of the staff nurses on the HDU, Shelagh, was very kind to me and could see that I was worried. She sat down next to my bed and explained in full detail what was happening to my heart. She even got a textbook from her office and showed me diagrams of the heart that I had not seen since studying human biology at school.

"Have I had a heart attack?" I asked.

"No, but your body is reacting in exactly the same way as if you have," she replied.

"This is serious stuff isn't it?" I can also remember saying to her, and she acknowledged that I was indeed very poorly.

Several days later one of Dr Lewis's team came to insert a central vein probe (CVP, a huge needle/probe) into my neck to monitor my heart movements. What seemed like an hour later I had this shooting pounding pain through my chest and up my body and I thought, Oh no, this time I really am having a heart attack! The next thing I felt a sharp stabbing and shooting pain in my head, which triggered the most almighty headache. Soon there were some doctors around my bed looking very concerned, and I can remember Dominic coming back to the hospital at that point and rubbing my head.

After a night when it had been touch and go, the sun did rise again in my lifetime and next morning while I was waiting for the nurses to distribute the breakfasts I looked down at my legs, which I have already said had been my best feature, and I thought to myself, Gosh, they look thin. I just thought that it was because they had not let me get out of bed for a couple of days, even to go to the loo. It's amazing what inactivity can do to your muscles, I thought, and I think I said to myself that I had seen better legs hanging out of a nest! Shelagh had already told me that on the HDU they worked very closely in conjunction with the staff on the coronary care unit.

"They know you are here and are keeping up to date with your progress," she said, then told me that they had decided to transfer me shortly to that ward, where I could have one-to-one nursing care.

Before I was moved to the CCU I had an awful experience with my boobs. My body was still producing milk, but my baby had effectively been taken away from me. My boobs became engorged with milk and were like huge rocks. Dom thought this was great, but I found it extremely painful. The nurses were kind and got me some cold saline bags to put inside my nursing bra. I would try and keep them in as long as I could before asking for some more cold bags straight from the fridge! All my visitors and the doctors who called at my bedside gave me very peculiar looks!

In my time on the CCU ward I had one-to-one nursing care and was really closely monitored. Again I quickly developed relationships with all the nurses, who were fantastic. I became especially close to two young nurses, both called Sharon, who were students at the time, and I used to really look forward to the days when they were on duty. They would really pamper me and do simple things like wash my hair, blow-dry it and get a radio for me to listen to. This was great at first, but then I became bored with the radio stations playing the same songs over and over again. Two tunes that really remind me of that awful time are *Pure and Simple* by Hearsay and a top tune by Toploader - *Dancing in the Moonlight*. I had really loved this second one, but came to dislike them both because of the memories associated with them and the chill that goes up my spine and around the back of my neck when I hear them now. I could not really concentrate enough to read my Michael Palin's *Around the World in Eighty Days* book or any other reading material, so I just used to watch the comings and goings on the ward.

When Dr Lewis's team came to see me they started to keep asking me strange questions. They would lift up my left leg and arm saying, 'Can you feel this?' as they scratched it with a silver medical implement. I asked Dom about this and he said something about a stroke. I questioned, 'Why didn't you tell me?' and he said that Dr Lewis had already done so. I did not recall, and I remember feeling shocked, completely devastated and thinking that only very old people have strokes and you can die from them! I now learned that the right side of my body was compensating for my left, and my muscles had wasted away. The stroke had occurred on a large portion of the right side of my brain, thus paralysing the whole of my left side. As a result of this, the nursing staff would not even let me get out of bed, as they were conscious that my heart was still in such a poor condition. I was totally and maybe blissfully unaware that I could in fact no longer walk because of muscle wastage and paralysis!

Another memory of being on that ward is that the nursing staff arranged for the dietician to come and see me to assess whether I could still eat! My appetite had completely gone, but she assessed me by getting me to drink a plastic cup of water. When doing this, she learned that the left side of my mouth was also paralysed and I would dribble a little bit, but when we tried food we also found out that I had not lost the ability to chew and swallow, although I kept getting food stuck in the side of my cheek like a squirrel storing food, and this again was down to muscle wastage of the left side of my face. This was news to me and I started to wonder what else had ceased to function!

The dietician instructed the nurses to only give me liquidised or soft food for a period. It was no wonder that my appetite did not come back for a while. Even Daniel wasn't eating pureed carrot yet, so why should I?

A few weeks later I felt quite positive about eating some breakfast and I asked to have some cornflakes, followed by

JANE COUPES

toast. The nursing staff told me that the dietician would not approve of this complex combination, but they would try me with this meal. I ate the cornflakes with no problems, using my right arm to feed myself. I then learned that it was impossible to put butter and jam on my toast with only one arm functioning properly. The toast flew about all over the tray, and I would defy anyone to open one of those little square packets of butter using just one arm. The nurses were on hand to help me and I think this was the first meal that I enjoyed since having my stroke.

As my appetite slowly returned, I would have this every morning for breakfast. Apparently the dietician was not happy that her advice had been ignored, so I had to have illegal and secretive cornflakes for the rest of my stay there!

The staff nurse on that ward was lovely and her name was Astrid, or Asteroid as one of her previous patients had called her. She was also very kind to me and she bought me some bottles of spring water to drink and also a lip balm. The reason for this was that I became very dehydrated because of some of the drugs I was taking, so my lips were all cracked at the sides. Dr Lewis had asked Astrid to instruct all the nurses to encourage me to drink lots of fluids. This seemed quite a difficult task at the time because I had become accustomed to the warm temperature in the hospital and I was not even moving much so could not really work up a thirst. I had experienced rapid weight loss after my stroke, so they tried to give me nutritional drinks to build up my body fat. They tasted foul and, although I would try to drink them, I found it very difficult. Throughout my working life my work colleagues used to comment on the fact that I hardly ever had a brew when one was made. I just used to have a cup of water from the vending machine and take small sips from it throughout the day.

Anyway, one of the nurses, whom I shall call Jenny Texas, was quite cruel to me, and every time she came into my room would bully me and ask if I had drank any of the drink. She said, 'We are doing this for your own good' and 'Your kidneys will pack up and you will die if you do not drink.' I wished she had sat down and explained properly what was happening to my body, which was that they were giving me tons of drugs effectively to dry my body out to stop another clot occurring, rather than trying the bullying tactics. Later on I joked to some of the other nurses that it was a good job I was so poorly, or I would have thrown the cup of liquid in her face.

My other outstanding memories of this time are as follows. I had been on the ward a while when I received some huge bunches of flowers. One was from my work colleagues at Barclays Bank, one from Ernst & Young, Dom's firm, and the other from a group of my girlfriends. They were all beautiful bunches and very colourful, and as I sat alone in my stark and brilliant white room, I visualised a raised platform with the flowers on. I thought that I could also see a piano or an organ and I thought to myself, gosh, this place is like the funeral parlour in the film, *My Girl*! In reality there was of course no raised platform; I must have been hallucinating. Dom later told me that they had been giving me the drug, Diamorphine, so this probably was the reason!

Another time, my friend, Maria, who was living in Reading back then, had been up to Stockport to visit her mum. Maria, her mum and Dom all came to visit me at the same time. I had been catching up with things going on in their lives. I remember that Maria wore a pale blue fleece, and a while after they had left and it was just me and Dom, I continued a conversation that I had been having with them.

"They went home ages ago!" Dom said.

I was adamant that I could still see Maria's blue fleece behind me at the top of my bed, and this was probably the first time I realised that my vision and spatial awareness had also been affected by the stroke!

Maria's mum, Therese, who is also Dom's auntie, brought me a present. This was a beautiful new pair of pyjamas made of blue and white checked material. They were from John Lewis and inside one of the pockets was a sample sachet of a perfume called Oscar De La Renta. I used to work with a girl called Cathy who wore this perfume and it immediately reminded me of her. I really liked it and used to dab a little on each wrist to make me feel a little better about myself.

One time, the nursing staff decided that I was well enough to have a shower instead of the endless bed baths I had been having. One of the nurses, Dawn, who I particularly liked, said she would assist me. I was stripped off and whisked down the corridor in a bath chair to the washrooms. When we got there the shower was very erratic and Dawn ended up having a better shower than I did. Her uniform was soaked and her shoes squelched back down the corridor to where her colleagues made fun of us both! I later became friendly with Dawn and she told me all about her own hospital experiences and about her children, who were quite a few years older than mine. I particularly remember that her daughter was due to go and see S Club 7 in concert later that year and Dom and I both said we could not wait until our children were old enough for all that stuff! It was kind of inevitable that we became friendly, as we had practically showered together!

The rest of the time on this ward, I was in a sort of daze and all I remember is that when the doctors did their daily rounds they kept having conversations within my earshot about my LV or left ventricular function and saying, 'She's tachycardic', which meant that my heart was beating too fast! It was a long time before I finally understood what they were talking about.

All Around Me

So far this has been my version of events, but I was so poorly they may be a little sketchy. To counter-balance this I have now included some accounts of that time, from people within my close circle of friends and family.

Both my mum and dad knew I was unwell after leaving hospital with Daniel and had also witnessed my deterioration until I ended up back in hospital with cardiomyopathy. On that fateful Thursday Dominic had phoned them to say that I had taken a dizzy turn and not to visit until the evening. They were surprised, as on the previous evening's visit they all thought I had made a big improvement. When Dominic and my mum and dad visited that evening en masse they were asked to wait in a small room off the ward whilst the sister arranged and urgently chased for a CT scan to be organised. At about 10 o'clock it was confirmed that I had had a stroke affecting about a third of the right side of my brain.

They were initially shocked to hear this information about my stroke. Dad says I looked like a sleeping princess, motionless with my hair laid out over the pillow. They were all devastated and in disbelief, as they said I looked so peaceful in my hospital bed. When Dominic asked the sister (or doctor) how ill I really was she replied:

"I notice that she is a Roman Catholic. Have you thought about contacting a priest?"

Her intention was that because I was so unwell a priest should give me the last rites (the sacrament of anointing). Dad calls to mind how many people across the area were praying for me including those of Christian, Muslim and Jewish faiths.

The first day I was admitted to hospital my mum and dad looked after Emily and Daniel. When Dominic eventually came to tell them the situation, he was emotional and visibly upset about me being wired up like a carburettor. Although devastated, he remained calm and collected, and drew Emily and Daniel close to himself. He wasn't happy to palm them off on other people and kept them with him as often as possible to restore our family unit.

As I lay on that bed on the HDU, my friend Michelle also lay resting on her bed. Tired and weary, the arrival, sleepless nights and constant breastfeeding of her twin girls, who had arrived six weeks before Daniel, had taken its toll. Her mum had come around to help with the babies, Abby and Erin, and in between tasks she answered the ringing telephone. It was Dom's cousin, Maria, to pass on the news. Michelle was shocked and worried for us all and as she had so recently had babies herself it very much brought things into perspective.

During my emergency care, I was too ill to see any visitors other than family, but Michelle recollects receiving daily updates as to my progress and writing a card to me, but having to word it carefully, as she was aware that I did not know the full extent of my condition. When visiting me on Ward A11,

Michelle said I looked lost, and still being very hormonal and post-natal herself, she burst into tears in her car on the journey home.

Completely 'stopped in his tracks' was how our friend Trevor described hearing the news of me being on the HDU. Whilst out and about shopping he had taken the call from Dom and immediately called his wife, Jane, to recount the story of what happened. Stunned and shocked, she wondered how something like this had gone undetected. Next came the news of my stroke, and Jane was unable to comprehend how a joyous occasion of delivering a bouncing, healthy, bonny baby boy could go so tragically wrong. They immediately offered their support to Dom, but felt totally helpless. Dom had told Jane that when any of our family members visited me for the first time, he had to prepare them for the shock of me wired up and so feeble.

Trevor and Jane keep in mind a time when they had invited Dom around to give him an hour's relief before he headed home by himself with Emily and Daniel.

"He was visibly very upset and looked absolutely lost to be honest!"

Jane gave Emily some tea. Her son, Ben, was already in bed, so Emily borrowed Ben's high chair. Trevor chatted to Dom then once Emily had been fed, they switched. Jane got upset too and gave Dom a big hug, reassuring him that they were there for him whenever he needed a release.

On a carefree birthday weekend trip to London, my college friend, Julia, was out shopping in Carnaby Street with her husband, and decided to ring Dom to find out how I was doing after my heart condition had forced me to be in hospital. She was completely traumatised to hear of my stroke and pregnancy complications, and also concerned, as she herself was pregnant with her second child, which was due in May. She recalls coming to visit whilst I was in Cherry Tree, and said I was there in body, but seemed to be almost in a trance-like state. For the first time ever she felt that I didn't really connect with her or giggle, which had been a terrible habit of ours during our college lectures! As the months rolled on Julia and some other girlfriends visited every Wednesday evening, sometimes with Julia's new baby, Antonia, in tow as one of the girls!

Our friends and neighbours, Trevor and Caroline, were on a skiing holiday at the time. When they returned there was a voicemail message on the landline answer phone from my primary school friend, Tanya. Her voice was cracking as she explained that I had been taken seriously ill. They both felt disbelief, shock and horror. They had called around only days before they left on their trip and Caroline commented to Trevor how we were the perfect family with a gorgeous little girl and a brand new, bouncing baby boy.

"You had everything going for you and then this thunderbolt struck out of the blue..."

"We could see that Dom was frantically busy, but despite this, he just seemed amazingly in control at all times. What a great pillar of strength to have by your side in times of crisis!"

Juggling a family and working can be tricky at the best of times. Suddenly having to take on extra responsibilities of looking after a newborn baby from 2 p.m. until 7 p.m., in addition to doing the school run, feeding, doing homework etc., was what my sister-in-law, Nicki, was only too pleased to do a couple of afternoons a week. My nephew and niece, Michael and Laura, have very strong memories of their mum at the school gates with their new baby cousin, Daniel, in tow. Up at 5 a.m. every morning, Nicki worked a shift in the bakery at Sainsbury's, returned home early afternoon to do some housework before driving to the hospital to collect Daniel and then straight to school to pick up her own children. It's no wonder that Daniel still has a very strong relationship with his Auntie Nicki, my brother's wife.

With time to kill on a long haul flight back from Australia to England, my Auntie Doreen was fed up to be leaving such a wonderful destination, another of her and my Uncle Dave's fantastic retirement trips, saddened to be returning to news that one of her close friends had died. Her thoughts turned to Daniel's birth, which she had already heard about during a phone call with her daughter, Jan, and this was to be her saving grace and jubilant news to return to. Having been on the other side of the world, she was unaware how events had unfolded, so once settled at home, she rang my mum to hear something cheerful, only to be told that I was now really poorly and back in Stepping Hill Hospital. Having spoken to her distraught sister, she got in the car and went around to my mum's house. She refused to believe how serious things were until she saw Dominic and his mum, Margaret, returning from the hospital where they had been waiting for news about my condition.

Down in Berkshire my cousin, Catherine, had delivered her baby boy, Jonathan, on 17th February, 2001, exactly one week before Daniel was born. My Auntie Connie had travelled down to offer some support, so my dad's brother, Tony, was home alone as he received the news. Both of them were completely devastated as they shared the news over the telephone, at the same time as imparting the latest joyful news about Catherine and Jonathan's progress.

Thinking about the time when Daniel and Jonathan were

babies evokes a strong memory of a time when Catherine came to visit me in hospital at Cherry Tree. We shared our news and chatted whilst in Room 3, and when it was time for Catherine and Jonathan to leave, we walked with our prams moving side by side along the corridors and to the main entrance where I waved them off. We chatted whilst walking out, and this again was a major breakthrough for me, although for me Daniel's pram was partly an aid for me to keep my balance whilst walking!

I met my friend Karen at a post-natal group in Marple after I had Emily and she had her son, Samuel. We are still friends just over nine years on. When Dominic searched through my mobile phone to get Karen's number to tell her the news that I was on the HDU, she immediately telephoned the local florist to order some flowers. During that conversation she insisted that my flowers were delivered that very same day as she wanted me to know that she had thought about me should the inevitable happen!

An unusual silence descended upon my doctor's surgery as the receptionists and other staff went about their work, where usually there were phones ringing and a general hustle bustle in a small village practice. I am related to two of the ladies managing the practice there at that time. One is my mother-in-law and the other Dom's Auntie Terry, and of course they were waiting for imminent news of my condition as were all the other staff.

Sitting in a line on the carpeted restaurant steps in The Three Cups pub in Stamford Bridge, York, ready for a photo opportunity, the three young girls wondered who would soon join their little group. They longed for another little girl to play with them. Emily loved going to visit Rachel and Natalie, our friends Dave and Elaine and their girls. It was approximately three days before my due date and we had seized the opportunity to visit for what might be a long time with a new baby on the scene. Days later the girls were slightly disappointed to hear that we had a boy and our friends were even more disappointed to learn of my illness, and because of work commitments they soon sent Dave's parents back over to their hometown of Stockport to visit me in hospital.

PART TWO
BACKGROUND

Northern Lights for a Northern Girl

I was born, Jane Victoria Philbin, at Stepping Hill Hospital in Stockport, Cheshire, on 31st December, 1968, yes, New Year's Eve. My dad says that I was born in a hurry and have been in a hurry ever since!

I would say that I had a mainstream working class childhood; probably very similar to most children growing up in the 1970s. Our influences at that time were from our favourite TV programmes such as *The A-Team, Starsky and Hutch, The Dukes of Hazzard* and *Champion The Wonder Horse,* so consequently we played lots of make-believe action-packed outdoor games. At that time I was probably a bit of a tomboy and played lots with Andrew and his friends, jumping off six-foot walls, climbing trees, riding our bikes in large groups (with our hoods up!) to play in Bramhall Park and play hide and seek in the woods, feed the fish and roll down the grass bank in front of the hall, kamikaze style!

During this period there were some defining and significant things that happened to me that would later shape the course of my life.

Me – 10 months

My earliest memory was when I went to see my primary school. I was to attend St Simon's RC Primary School in Hazel Grove. My brother, Andrew, who is three years older, was already there, had lots of friends and was enjoying school life.

As I was to start after Christmas, I went to have a look around the school. It was all open-plan and they were in the middle of a huge refurbishment programme, as they were separating the infants from the juniors with some huge glass fire doors. I remember mum took me, and there was still plastic sheeting everywhere around the school and still even some workmen working in the school grounds. There were several square areas dotted around, which were separated by curtains that could be drawn when privacy was required to form a classroom. My favourite games at school were playing kiss chase and *Charlie's Angels* (a popular TV programme of the time). The other girls used to argue about who was playing the characters Kris and Kelly, but I was always happy to be Sabrina anyway, as she was still very attractive, but was also the clever one who solved all the crimes.

I remember starting school and sitting at hexagonal tables with little chairs. I soon made friends with Tanya, Emma, Katrina and some of the boys too; David Laing, Simon Tinning and Douglas King. I especially liked story time when we went into the square areas, drew the red psychedelic curtains and had a story read to us. The female teachers used to choose four children, two who were allowed to draw a curtain each once we were all sitting cross-legged on the floor, and two others (girls usually) who were allowed to play with the teacher's hair. A few of the female staff members had beautiful long hair and we were allowed to take turns combing it, playing with it, and putting clips and bobbles in it, whilst the story was read. My favourite teachers were Miss Lahan, Mrs O'Gara, Mrs Smith and Miss Sellars.

During the summer term we had endless games of baseball, and I always played fourth base and enjoyed stumping people out. I also started to play netball and was good enough to play in the goal attack position on our school team. I occasionally played goal shooter too, but I didn't like the rule where you had to stay in your third of the court and couldn't really get involved in the rest of the game.

Once we played in a tournament at Our Lady's School in Edgeley. We got to the final and ended up playing St Joseph's,

Reddish team, who were notoriously good at netball in our local area. I missed a vital goal and felt bad, but my team knew I had not been on form that day. A return match was arranged, but this time it was a home game for us and we were fired up to show our true colours. We ended up thrashing them about 20-0 and I got quite a few goals. One of my last goals, the ball spun around the rim a few times before falling into the net. There was a huge cheer, and as we walked to get changed, my team reminded me that I had come good in the end, even though I felt I had let them down in the tournament. As this had been such a vital game, some of the boys had stuck around after school to watch. I was pleased that some of them had cheered us on and my performance and goals had been noticed.

Always lively, a petite girl with blonde pigtails, I also attended Brownies outside school and because of my impish behaviour was put into the Imps pack. I remember going after lots of badges for the sleeves of my brown uniform and in particular doing work for my hostess badge. For this I went to an older Brownie's house and her mum gave me tasks to complete like setting the table with plates, cutlery, flowers, condiments etc., washing up and some other domestic chores.

I will never forget one particular Thinking Day at Brownies. One 22nd February (in 1976, as I guess I was about eight and had not been in the Brownies that long) we had our Thinking Day ceremony in the Brownie hall. Sitting cross-legged in a circle, which had a huge map of the world in the centre, we all had a line to say.

"I'm thinking about Brownies in..."

We all had a particular country to name then had to light a tea light candle and place it in the centre of the circle. I think you probably have an inkling what's coming next! When it

JANE COUPES

was my turn to light my candle, I lit the match and struggled to light the tea light as it had a faulty wick on it. My match still had a flame, which was slowly flickering up the matchstick closer to my thumb. I stupidly didn't let the match go as the Brownie hall had an old wooden floor and I was very aware that we could all go up in flames. I finally shook the match frantically from side to side and the flame went out, but I wasn't in time to stop burning the end of my thumb. I had a huge white blister on the end of it for weeks, and struggled to hold my pencil whilst writing at school! Consequently, I was terrified of fire and matches for a very long time.

My extra-curricular activities continued and I also went to gymnastics after school one evening each week, and was always doing cartwheels, handstands or 'tippling' as my mum still says. Now my daughter, Emily, does it! On these evenings we had to stay later at school, so had to let the school bus go without us, consequently, we were allowed to get the public 192 bus home. We went in a small group; Andrew and me together with Tanya and her brother, Simon. In order to get to the bus stop for the 192 bus on the main A6 road, we had to walk across the grounds of Chapel Street School and we always seemed to be chased by a fierce Dalmatian dog, of which Tanya and I were terrified.

On Saturdays we often went swimming, and Dad worked hard to ensure that Andrew and I were strong and confident swimmers. Andrew was even good enough to swim for the school team. We both did backstroke and once I was picked for the school team, but never actually competed, as I was ill on the day of the gala.

After lunch, Dad always tested us on our spellings and we were really competitive, trying to answer each other's questions, and this was also one of the times when we practised our recorders. The one and only tune we could play was 'Good King Wenceslas', so I'm sure Mum and Dad got fed up with it! However, the recorder music was pay back for their records of The Carpenters, Burt Bacharach, Nat King Cole and Johnny Mathis, which Andrew and I sometimes tired of!

Sundays meant going to church at St Peter's RC Church, again in Hazel Grove, and our school shared this church with St Peter's RC School, which was across the main A6 road. I enjoyed going to church, as we got to see our school friends away from our school environment. We lived on the edge of the school catchment area. Most of our friends lived in Hazel Grove, consequently, we only saw them at school or church. We went with Dad and nearly always sat upstairs in the balcony where the choir sat. We were usually a little late and left a little early, so that we could go and see Granddad.

My dad's father, Lawrence, was one of our only two surviving grandparents and we doted on him. He lived in Edgeley on Larkhill Road. This was in a hilly part of Stockport and we had to drive down a steep hill to get to his house. At the back of his terraced house there was a back entry and then a lean-to garage where Granddad parked his white Hillman Imp. There was a gate that was always padlocked. When you went through there was an extremely steep set of concrete steps leading to his garden that had a vegetable patch and a big patio area, which had a brilliant panoramic view of Stockport. Trees now obscure this view, but there is a huge motorway network there and a glass pyramid that belongs to The Co-op Bank. We liked helping Granddad tend to his vegetables, lettuces and tomatoes that he used to grow, always in straight lines! He used to tell us old war stories and tales about his family. He also did card tricks for us and we had

JANE COUPES

endless games of patience with him. He could manipulate a pack of playing cards whereby you divide them into two and then flick them together, thus shuffling them. Andrew and I were highly impressed and tried to practise this to perfection, without success.

Granddad was one of seven children and so was my nana. He always went on holiday with his only surviving brother, Vincent, to Ireland to see his late wife's family. They lived in a place called Clonmel, County Tipperary, on the south-east coast of Ireland, and when he returned he always brought us some white pudding back as a gift.

One time when they went they arranged to take Andrew and my cousin, Paul, with them. My cousin, Catherine, and I were too young, so had to stay at home and we felt a bit miffed. They brought back loads of fabulous photographs of adventures they had had, plus they had met all Nana's family over there. She had died when I was very young and I feel a little bit sad that I do not really remember her. She sounded a fascinating woman.

Her name was Johanna, and I understand she was a quietly spoken Irish woman who had an extraordinary understanding of people and life. Whilst my granddad was in the Royal Air Force, she took her three children (my dad, John, his brother, Tony, and sister, Frances) to live in Ireland, to care for her mother, who was ill with cancer. She took them single-handedly, luggage and all, via bus, train and boat, which must have been quite a journey with three young children during wartime regulations. When her mother died she brought them back to the UK to live in Middleton Junction, Manchester, and brought them up until Granddad returned from the Far East at the end of the war. My dad tells a story that when she broke her finger she cut the plaster cast off with a bread knife before the recommended time that she was supposed to remove it! This was mainly because it was getting in her way and she didn't want to return to hospital.

Minnie and Stanley Hadfield were my mother's parents whom I also never knew. My mum's mother, Minnie, died in her late twenties due to an outbreak of scarlet fever in the family. It was particularly sad at the time, as she died on Christmas Eve in the Lake Isolation Hospital in Ashton. My mum was only four at the time, and she and her father went to live with her grandparents in Pine Street, Brinksway, Stockport.

After the war my mum's father, Stanley, married a war widow, Edie Burton, whose soldier husband had been killed in the Gaza Strip. Mum instantly had an older sister, Doreen, and they all moved as a family into a terraced house at 55 Brinksway, Stockport. They later moved to a semi-detached house in Lorland Road, Cheadle Hulme, and it was there that we used to visit my mum's step-mum. We always seemed to call at Saturday teatime, and Nana liked to watch the wrestling on the television. Andrew used to pretend to wrestle me to the floor and beat me up all the time. As he got older, he tried judo at Bramhall Leisure Centre and used to come home and say 'Look what I've just learnt', as he threw me over his shoulder.

Dad worked hard and long hours. He worked for ICL in West Gorton, in management. As we got older, Mum took a job at the local secondary school across the road as a domestic. Financially, I don't think she needed to take a job, but she just wanted a bit of extra cash and independence for herself and to treat us. Mum worked split shifts and Dad gave us breakfast until she was able to come back from work in the mornings and help us get our uniforms on and walk us down to the bus stop.

Our nearest stop for the school bus was outside the convent school on the A6, and all the mums used to stand around chatting and smoking (which was socially acceptable then) while we waited for our bus. I felt important when it was my turn to have the money to pay the driver. The fare was 2p and I remember feeling very grown-up when I handed over the money and said:

"Two twos, please."

Mum used to smoke in Dad's car and both Andrew and I hated it and vowed we would never smoke ourselves. We had an orange Ford Marina. Dad used to change his car quite often and we loved going to the car showrooms to look for our new vehicle.

Mum's job meant that she wasn't there when we got home from school, but that was fine. We soon learned to be streetwise and cross the main road safely after getting off the bus. This was with assistance from the Green Cross Code, and then we headed to the school where Mum worked. Sometimes the caretaker would unlock the gym and let us use the equipment (ropes, vaults etc) whilst our mums finished their duties.

As the years rolled by, when we got home, Andrew was in charge until Mum or Dad got home at around 6 p.m. and the responsibility went to his head. He got a bit power crazy and would try and boss me around lots and say what snacks we were allowed before tea and when I had to do my homework. I wasn't happy about being bossed around and often made it known.

~

In 1977 it was the Queen's Jubilee and she drove down the stretch of the A6 road near us. We waited outside the newsagents and caught a glimpse of her in her black state car. We also had a street party in Coombes Street. Everyone brought out their pasting tables that were used when wallpapering the house and we decorated them with red, white and blue streamers.

Early that morning my dad caught our paper boy trying to steal a large Union Jack flag that was in the middle of our bunting that we had used to decorate the street. All the mums went to a lot of effort to make nice snacks, and the dads drank beer! Our party was going well and then we heard a siren. Next minute a fire engine drove into our street. It turned out someone had left an electrical item on and started a small house fire. Once they had put the fire out and checked there was minimal damage, the firemen parked their engine near the brick wall and we all sat on its bumper while the mums offered the firemen some of our snacks.

~

In 1978, at the age of ten I went on a school trip from St Simon's School to Norway. Our headmaster had been on a trip over there and had become friendly with a local head teacher. The trip was supposed to be an exchange, but in actual fact we went to visit over there and for some reason they never came to England to stay with us.

This was my first time away from my parents properly. Mum and Dad had been away for weekends, but we always stayed with my granddad and Auntie Frances. She never married and still lived with my granddad in Edgeley. One

JANE COUPES

memorable time when they looked after us was when Mum and Dad went to Brussels around Easter time for a weekend break. Before the weekend began, Mum and Dad had taken me shopping for a new pink jacket for the summer. Andrew and I began the weekend at Granddad's house, where we enjoyed the different taste of toast on a gas grill rather than our modern electric one and staying in strange beds up Granddad's extremely steep stairs, but we didn't particularly enjoy having to use his outside toilet - in the freezing cold weather!

After church on that Sunday, Granddad and Auntie Frances decided to take us back to our own house, as we getting a little bored away from our own toys. We were allowed to stop at the newsagents for Granddad to buy his Sunday paper, and Andrew and I were treated to a cream egg each. Andrew devoured his immediately. I wanted to savour mine later, so put it safely in my pocket.

Granddad always drove his white Hillman Imp at speed and as he hurtled around the corner near our house, Auntie Frances, who was not a small lady, was thrown across the car and sat on my pocket! Yes, the cream egg was no more and my new pink coat was all sticky and in need of a good wash, consequently, I couldn't wear it again for ages. Andrew thought this highly hilarious and said that it served me right and something along the lines of:

"What kind of a weirdo saves chocolate anyhow?"

Also during that weekend, Auntie Frances turned on one of the taps in our bathroom and the top of the tap broke off. When Mum and Dad returned they couldn't get a replacement with a letter 'C' on it and to this day the taps in Mum and Dad's bathroom still both have an 'H' on them, although they do in fact have both hot and cold running water!

Anyway, back to Norway. I was very excited about the prospect of going on an aeroplane, but even more so as I would be with my friends. We caught a London train from Edgeley Station, where our parents waved us off. When we arrived at Heathrow Airport it seemed vast to us and at first we tried to check in at the wrong terminal. We eventually made our way to the correct terminal - a feat in itself with twenty plus ten year olds dragging heavy suitcases. As we ran across the terminal, we heard our parties' name being called over the tannoy.

"This is the final call for passengers on flight No --- to Stavanger Airport."

We just made it in time. The flight was very exciting and when we arrived in Norway we still had to catch a hydrofoil to the island where we were staying with families, which was called Bokn Island. Around this time I had started my fascination with polar bears. I thought my cuddly toys were fluffy and cuddly, but I was also intrigued by the majestic, but ferocious, polar bears, so started to collect polar bears in any shape or form.

I loved Norway. It was very clean and the people were very friendly. We finally boarded the boat to get to Bokn and it was a beautiful journey along the fjords. I found it breathtaking even at such an early age and thoroughly enjoyed the experience of being away from home.

We eventually arrived on Bokn Island and as we got off the boat onto the jetty, a brass band from the local school met us and played a tune. These were the children whose families we would be staying with and we looked excitedly to see who might be our own new friend. I immediately spotted a girl who looked nice. She was marching next to a gorgeous boy with blond hair. As we arrived up the hill at the school, this boy held the door open for us and I'm not sure about everyone else, but he gave me a lovely smile as we went through. It was finally the end of our long, but hurried, journey and we sat down to have a meal, a hot meat stew, and afterwards we sang them a friendship song that we had learned in Norwegian. As I write this, I can still hear the song in my head, even though the words are foreign and I do not speak Norwegian; 'Og mannen hag lech' seg y ved afrog, Hi farrah, y ved a frog!'

When we met our family I was pleased. There were two of us staying with them, as they had such a fantastic and large house. My friend, Tracy Jones, and I stayed with them. The Kristiansund family were lovely. There were seven children - Kristin, Heidi, Evan, Ivan and some little ones. We drove to their house, which was a short drive from the school. It was in an idyllic setting and they even had their own boat that their father was restoring. I thought their wooden house was an upside-down house, as it was on the side of a hill and the living area was upstairs and the bedrooms downstairs.

We had lots of adventures during our week. Kristin was very friendly with the gorgeous boy with blond hair, Vieglake, and as he lived close by we all played together all week. He was paired up with Simon Tinning from my school and we were good pals anyway. One of the older girls from our school, Cheryl Rushworth, was staying on a completely different island to us. She had another boat ride to West Bokn, whereas we were staying on Oustre Bokn, or East Bokn, and we had to wave her off on her extended journey!

My highlights of the week were helping the family to restore the boat and painting it. At the end of the week it was finished and they named it *Tracy Jane*, after their guests. We fried sausages on an open fire on a beach in a place called

Luton, on the other side of the island. We went on a day trip back to Stavanger, bought presents for our families back home and went in an expensive café bar for lemonade. We had already brought traditional English gifts from home, like Wedgewood pottery, for our Norwegian families. I also liked reading my letters from home. We were not allowed to ring home on this trip, but our parents had written us letters, pretending they were full of current news, which we could open during our break.

One evening whilst playing near the boat, I reckon we happened upon a filtered, but very colourful and spectacular version, of The Northern Lights (like a red and green amazing and captivating laser show, which filled the whole sky), which has left me with a very strong desire to visit Norway again.

~

Summer times meant no school, old Elvis films on the television in the mornings and *Why Don't You* (a popular children's series after which Andrew and I would try to perfect very strong regional accents with some success!) and walks down to the sweet shop at the bottom of Lake Street, where we could buy penny chews in a paper bag. Out of school I liked playing with Andrew and his friends, and was probably a bit of a tomboy, jumping off six-foot walls, climbing trees, chasing, but also playing with my Sindy dolls together with their Action Men etc.

On Coombes Street where we lived there were lots of other children, mostly girls of my age. They all went to the local school, Great Moor, and I sometimes felt a little left out as I went to a Catholic school in Hazel Grove. I still played with them lots in our street and cemented some firm and

JANE COUPES

lasting friendships, but more often that not I would play with Andrew and his friends.

When I was three or four we had a lovely late holiday in Bournemouth. The weather was absolutely fantastic and Andrew and I used to play in the sea every day with some friends we had made. One of our favourite pastimes was to lie in the sea in the shallow water and we would all lift our arms up and point to the sky as the waves trickled around us. The holiday seemed to go on forever and we were all sad when the two-week break came to an end and we returned home.

About a fortnight later Mum said that as the weather was still so good, we were going out for the day to see the Blackpool illuminations. We decided to picnic on the beach at St Anne's, have some tea and in the evening drive through the lights at Blackpool. Mum says everything went well and we had a good trip there and parked next to the beach. Having picked our spot, Andrew and Dad went back to the car to collect our deckchairs and cool box. Whilst they were arranging everything apparently I disappeared. Panic stricken, Mum, Dad and Andrew scanned and searched the beach with their eyes and, although there were only a few people dotted on the beach, I was nowhere to be seen. Mum and Dad can't help laughing when they remember what happened next. Their panic increased, as they couldn't locate me and quite a time had elapsed. As Dad looked out to sea he saw a pair of tiny arms rising slowly out of the sea. I was playing the very same game that we had played in Bournemouth weeks before, only this time I was fully clothed! Everyone was so relieved that I was safe, although completely soaked, and I must have been the only girl to drive through the illuminations that evening wearing my unused swimming costume and wrapped in my brother's anorak!

Some years later when Andrew was eight and I was five, we had another great holiday, this time in Weymouth. The weather was scorching and everyone was on the beach. On the first day Dad bought us a small rubber dinghy and told us to be very careful and stay near the edge of the sea. Andrew met another boy called Andrew and we all had lots of fun every day, playing at the edge of the sea with Mum and Dad taking turns in looking to see that we were okay.

For two weeks the weather had been lovely, hot and very settled. On the last day I was playing at the edge of the sea with the two Andrews in the dinghy and all of a sudden there was a great gust of wind and the dinghy was swept out to sea with the two Andrews in it. My dad had seen this and rushed down to where I was, now alone by the edge of the water. Dad looked around and decided to run to the pier where the dinghy was heading. As he got halfway there, people were standing up and pointing at the dinghy and quite a crowd had gathered on the beach. A teenager with a pedalo said he would go and rescue them. He was a strapping young boy and soon got out to the dinghy. Dad was pacing up and down the beach waiting for them to return and says all he could hear were the people on the beach, not knowing who he was, saying:

"Where were the parents?"

"Some parents don't care"

"Wouldn't you think they would look after their kids better?"

Needless to say, that was the last time we used the dinghy on *that* holiday. We used it on many later holidays, but had learned a lesson the hard way.

I vividly remember Dad buying our first colour television. He was quite ahead of his time back then, and my uncle and some of Dad's friends came around to watch the FA Cup Final in colour. Mum loved tennis and for two weeks every June, she seemed glued to our television watching Bjorn Borg and John McEnroe. When it was our turn to watch television, Andrew and I watched shows such as, *The A-Team, Starsky and Hutch, The Dukes of Hazzard, Zorro* and *Champion the Wonder Horse.*

One thing for sure was that our house was never short of laughs. Andrew has always been a bit of a joker and done silly things to get laughs, including flicking the tea towel at my and Mum's legs until we howled with laughter and pain, and doing an impression of the Swedish chef from *The Muppet Show,* The Count from *Sesame Street* and also Scooby Doo!

As I grew older, I started getting invited out to tea to my friends' houses. I went to Tanya's, ate pizza for the first ever time and felt very continental. On another trip to Tanya's, we paraded the streets near her house in Davenport in our leotards, pretending we were good enough to be championship gymnasts. I went to Emma's house and we played in the garden and took her huge lop-eared rabbit for a walk on a lead, and I went to Katrina's for a sleepover and we sang into our hairbrushes to music. A song that was out then was Buggles with the song, 'Video Killed the Radio Star', and Katrina and I had a little dance routine to the song whilst singing into our hairbrushes.

As my birthday was in December, straight after Christmas, I usually took a few friends to the pantomime at the Davenport theatre near us as my birthday treat. More often than not we went to a matinee performance and came back (often making footprints in the snow) for a party tea at my house. In the circle upstairs they had big comfy double chairs, where two people could sit together and watch the show, and we usually booked one of those along with our tickets, so I could choose one of my best friends to sit next to me. The Davenport had one of those Wurlitzer organs that came up on a platform during the interval with coloured lights, and I thought it was great.

~

It was now summertime and you could usually find our branch of the Philbin family packing up the car and driving to Tenby to stay in a caravan, or to Bournemouth to stay in a small family-run bed and breakfast. Andrew and I loved both holidays, and I particularly remember our caravan holidays and us arguing over who was allowed to walk to the camp shop by ourselves to get sausages, bread and milk in the mornings before breakfast.

In Bournemouth there were steep paths with steps that ran down to the beach called The Chimes. During one holiday, every time I walked down the steps in my flip-flops I stubbed my toe on a step, so that by the end of our week it was a bloody mess and had to be bandaged up!

~

During the same year as my Norway trip (1978), I was playing out in the street with my girlfriends when a van pulled up outside our house and a man got out and came over.

"Is this the house that's for sale?" he asked.

I looked at him, puzzled.

"Definitely not."

He drove off with a smile on his face and we continued with our game.

When I went in for lunch, I asked Mum and Dad about it and they said that in fact, yes, they had decided we were moving, not far, but we were to move to a brand new house that was being built nearby. Later that afternoon, the man came back with his van. He took out a wooden For Sale sign and knocked it into the ground outside our house, after glancing over at us and smirking.

Andrew and I were a little stunned, but also excited, and we asked to go and look at the new house. Mum and Dad only had limited details about our new house, but it felt like it was going to be a good move. However, it was the end of an era for us and also the start of a new adventure.

Me & Andrew on the pier at Bournemouth - 1975

High School Connection

Once we found out exactly where our new house was being built, Andrew and I became all inquisitive and decided to go and have a look with our friends. The house was being built on a site where there used to be an outdoor swimming pool in Stockport (not sure why, as Stockport is not renowned for its tropical climate!), called The Blue Lagoon. We decided not to go on our bikes and walked around the corner on our curious adventure.

There was a huge fence at the entrance to the building site, but we discovered that you could pull back a section of it and sneak through. We went in and found a shed that looked quite interesting. It had been used as a pay desk when the pool had been open, but there were still some chairs and a desk in it, so we thought it would make a good den/base whilst we explored the site, which didn't seem to have a lot of building work going on at the moment.

There was also a derelict building that had been the changing facilities, toilets and a café, which we explored and you could even walk around the edge of the original pool, now full of murky water with frogs in it. The builders had dismantled some of the blue water slides and they had been left around the edges of the pool. Our exploration sessions went on for a few weeks and we made our den very homely with items borrowed from our house - we even had soft drinks and sweets in there, but these were always kept to a minimum stock in case someone found our stash.

One afternoon we went to spend some more discovery time and there were loads of workmen about and the foreman barked at us, chased us and told us to get off his site. The next time we returned our shed had been ripped down and our den was demolished.

Andrew and I had wanted to tell the foreman that we actually had some right to be there as our mum and dad had bought one of the new houses, but we never got the chance. He just thought we were disruptive and meddling kids who were trespassers, but we were really just inquisitive. Even at this early foundation stage, we argued about who was having what room!

Close to our new house there was a dirt track that ran alongside a huge field. This was our open space where we used to explore, play games and hang out. It was actually the playing field shared by a couple of local secondary schools. Over the huge, red brick wall at one edge of the playing field were some trees and an old derelict hospital.

It was also around this time that I had to make what I now know was my first major decision. Mum and Dad asked me which secondary school I wanted to go to when I left St Simon's that summer. I couldn't take the easy route and follow Andrew to St James's School (where he later became deputy head boy), as that had now moved from the old convent building at the bottom of our road to a brand new building in Cheadle Hulme, which was out of our catchment area. The choices I was left with were St Ann's School in Heaton Chapel and Harrytown RC High School in Romiley.

Most of my close friends had already made their momentous decisions and at the time the places were awarded by the local education authority, I was the one and only girl from St Simon's going to Harrytown School. For the first time ever I really did feel in a quandary. I recall crying floods of tears in my bedroom and Dad came up to see me. He told me that we could go to look around both schools before I made my mind up, but he also felt it would be easier for me to settle into any new school if I had my friends around me. Consequently, we appealed and therefore...

My first memory of starting at Harrytown School was having my picture taken in our back garden in my new uniform before I got on our school bus, the 803. Once I arrived there, all the new first years in our pristine uniforms, had to meet up in the dining hall. There we met Mr Darke, who was Welsh. He was to be our year head, but also taught metalwork at the school. He always used to shout, 'stand in a straight line' at the top of his voice, and this sentence had much more than a twang of his Welsh accent in it! His instructions on that first day were that we had to sit tight until our name was called out then we would be divided up into form groups.

There were five classes in each year and they each had a letter; 'H', 'T', 'O', 'W' and 'N' (short for Harrytown, of course). I waited patiently and it seemed that all my friends from St Simon's (thankfully there were some in the end!) had been allocated a form group. Tanya was in 'N' and Katrina and Emma were in 'T'.

JANE COUPES

Eventually my name was called out and I was with at least one other girl from my primary school in 'W' form. She was called Paula James and I had been quite friendly with her at St Simon's. I had also been for tea at Paula's house and we had a disco, complete with our rah-rah skirts, in her converted cellar. Her dad was a real DJ at night and had heaps of records. He also had his own shop that sold hi-fis and electrical items. Also Simon Tinning was in our class, so we thought we would be okay - safety in numbers and all that.

My time at Harrytown School was happy. I was doing well in all my subjects and had a large network of friends. I worked extremely hard and put in a lot of effort, especially in maths, a subject at which I didn't feel naturally gifted! This was around the time when I first noticed that sometimes in life there are people who don't necessarily put in the effort, but still get exemplary results at exam/test times. It felt unfair, but just made me work harder and put in more effort. My favourite subjects then were English, history and French, as I really liked our teacher, Mr Want. He made the lessons come alive. We covered the work that was necessary, but also had a laugh with him. I think several of the girls also had a crush on him and one Sunday morning in April we went to cheer him on as he ran the Stockport Marathon.

Our form teacher for our first year was to be Mrs Medina. We thought she looked a little bit like a witch, with long grey hair and a wart on her face. She had a son, Robbie, in the year above us and she also had other children, who were younger and they had also attended St Simon's school. Our classroom was at the front of the school and looked out on the main road where the bus stops were. The school was huge after St Simon's and I sometimes felt daunted following my new timetable and trying to be in the right classroom at the right time.

Directly opposite our school was Bredbury Comprehensive School and sometimes there were fights at hometime between our older boys and theirs.

I enjoyed playtime, but can remember being scared when I needed the loo. The toilets were down a set of stairs off the playground and they were quite dirty. When you went in there, there were lots of older girls smoking.

When we were in our first year, the current fourth year class was the first ever mixed-sex class in the school, as before that it had been a girls only school run by nuns. I thought the fourth year pupils were really hip and trendy. There was a song in the charts at the time called 'Reward' by The Teardrop Explodes and the fourth year used to sing it at the top of their voices and pretend to do the trumpet fanfare at the top of the steps.

There was a boy in my class who was very tall with dark hair, and he was totally into sport. He was also one of a handful of people in our year who could fully complete the Rubik's cube. I had already checked him out and thought he was mighty fine. His name was Dominic Coupes. He and his friend, Robert Gall, both from St Mary's School in Marple Bridge, used to sit in front of Paula and me in our form class. We had a good laugh with them when they weren't talking about football. They were really friendly with some boys who were in class 'O'; Dave Lynch (the class joker), Trevor Shepherd (the only eleven year old I have ever met who already had a moustache and streaked hair!) and Trevor Martin (who had been a good friend of Dom's from St Mary's since they were four).

Dom's cousin, Maria, tells a story around the time that

Dom and I first set eyes on each other. I was eleven, but he was only ten, as he is nine months younger than me. He was one of the youngest in our school year, but also one of the brightest.

One day quite a crowd had congregated in our form room. We were all chatting before lessons. Maria walked in, put her elbows down on Dominic's desk, leaned into him and started chatting. My friends, Paula, Katrina and a few others, saw this and called her a nasty name. They knew I had set my sights on Dom, so were quite defensive on my behalf at this girl who was showing him all this attention. What we discovered later is that they were first cousins and had practically been brought up like brother and sister as part of a huge family.

When I realised that Maria wasn't a threat, we became good friends and used to sit next to each other in some classes, as we were in the same maths stream, top set - although I'm not quite sure how I got in there, as I was always better at English, French and history.

Our maths teacher was Mrs Lee. She was very tall and had her hair in a long salt and pepper grey bob. It was always so straight that sometimes I thought it looked a bit like a helmet. Mrs Lee's maths lessons were in a long classroom at a deserted end of a corridor up near the science labs. In our very first lesson with her, at the very beginning she wrote '1985' in huge numbers on the blackboard.

"This is what we are aiming towards," she said. "1985 is the year when you will all sit your O levels, and the time between now and then is preparation time to cover all the topics required."

She was very driven and her lessons were always at a fast pace.

One time when Maria was sitting next to me, she asked Mrs Lee for some paper as she had run out. Mrs Lee stormed off to the very back end of the classroom and came back with a whole ream of paper still wrapped in cellophane and plonked it down on Maria's desk.

"Don't interrupt me when I am in full flow," she would say at any interruption.

Sometimes I would ask her to repeat something if I was struggling (usually quadratic equations!) and she would say to me:

"You can come back at lunchtime or after the lesson and I will go through it with you."

To both Maria's questions and mine, she would always say:

"Don't interrupt me. I want to keep these boys on track for fantastic marks in their O levels."

She would then point over to where Dom, Dave, Andrew Chatterton, Simon Tinning and a few others sat!

~

I was thirteen when I first managed to get together with Dominic. We had our first kiss at St Peter's disco. I was thirteen and he was twelve. At the time he was supposedly 'going out' with my friend, Louise Dunne. 'Going out' with someone meant that you ended up necking with them at the end of any house parties that went on, ignored them the rest of the time and as a pair you were the brunt of lots of girlfriend/boyfriend jokes in the playground. Our first kiss was at the end of the evening and it was really nice. When I awoke the following morning I was riddled with guilt that I had kissed my friend's boyfriend.

There was a bit of animosity between Louise and me for a

few days and I was called nasty names by some of the other girls, but it didn't last for long and we were friends again and she was still with Dom as his official girlfriend! However, as far as I was concerned that kiss was it for now, but I really did like Dom and a seed had been sown!

During one of our summer holidays I arranged to go swimming with some friends to Jacksons Lane Swimming Pool. We met in Hazel Grove and went into a shop, and one of the girls brought ten Benson & Hedges cigarettes and four packets of polo mints. They had decided we should try smoking, as we were now teenagers. I was really naive and just thought we were going swimming, so was a bit shocked when as we were walking down a path that ran adjacent to the railway line, they both lit their cigarettes and started smoking. They asked me if I wanted to have a go and I wasn't really sure, but decided to give it a go anyway. I put the cigarette in my mouth and immediately started coughing really badly. Smoking obviously was not for me. At least now I had tried it and dismissed it, I didn't feel so excluded when most of the other girls in my class were smoking.

I was never one to bow to peer pressure anyway, but also I had a few health concerns of my own that became apparent around that time. When I ate meals I started to get terrible stomach pains on my right-hand side. I guess it was also around this time that I became aware of my self-image. I had a little bit of puppy fat, but wanted to be slim and curvy like some of the other girls in my class. As a result of the tummy pains, I started to eat less and less, and began skipping meals when I could.

By the latter end of my time at Harrytown I went really thin and was wrongly diagnosed with anorexia, when I really had symptoms of Crohn's disease that went undetected. I don't believe I ever really was anorexic, but I was in so much pain after eating food that I did get into that thing whereby you hide food, skip meals etc. Mum and Dad asked the school nurse to check on me at mealtimes to ensure I was eating my sandwiches and not throwing them in the bin near the bus stop. A couple of times I fainted in church and Dad had to carry me out.

We went to a meeting in Salford for girls who were anorexic and I remember thinking, I just have a problem with my stomach; I know that I'm way too thin. When we went to the meeting Mum and Dad went into one room with all the other parents and I entered a different room with the other girls. They talked about looking in a mirror and seeing a horrendously fat person when they were skinnier than I was. I could even see one of the other girl's ribs through her skin. I totally did not associate with this, as I saw that I was too thin and just wanted to get back to eating properly without the horrible pain.

Nevertheless, I would still describe my time at Harrytown School as happy, and some memorable times were as follows.

~

"Jane, you're so slight that I'm sure you'll pick up some nuclear radiation while we're exploring," were the words Mr Lees uttered as our coach sped along the M56 motorway to North Wales.

We were on our fourth year geography field trip to Dinorwig Nuclear Power Station in Gwynedd. The word on the coach was that when we had completed a tour of the power station, we had to go through an elaborate security system that checked to see if any of us had picked up any nuclear energy whilst we were in there. If this was the case then you had to live in the power station for the rest of your life and you would never see your family again. The trip was quite interesting. We split into groups, completed our worksheets and marvelled at the fact that we were underground, inside a mountain, like something out of a James Bond film.

True to Mr Lees' word, when I filed through the buzzer system on the way out, the alarms sounded in a way that I imagine alarms went off during the Second World War when there was a threat of bombs. I heard a whisper in the crowd of children craning their necks to see what the excitement was.

"Jane Philbin isn't coming back with us on the coach, as she was contaminated!"

I was utterly terrified. How could I have picked up nuclear radiation? I wanted to see my family again! After a few attempts at going through the buzzer system, they let me get back on the coach and after that I never liked Mr Lee as much, as I felt that he had performed some weird voodoo curse on me. Before the trip I had thought he was a good teacher who held our attention.

It was different to be in fourth year because then our classroom was 'the hut'. Our local education authority was obviously short of cash, because our classroom ('the hut') was literally a wooden decrepit construction situated on a piece of land between the new buildings and the old convent buildings, which were haunted if you listened to the older pupils.

〜

In the fifth year (1984) we went on a skiing trip to Les Deux Alps in France. We flew to Grenoble and began our ski school. We had a fantastic time. The song 'Last Christmas' by Wham was climbing the charts around this time and the video was set in a snowy place, so that set the scene for our holiday.

One particular night that stands out in my memory was when all the lads in our group got stuck in the lift in our apartment. Too many had got in at once and they ended up being rescued by firemen, as the lift got stuck in the lift shaft between floors. All the girls in our party were concerned for our friends and potential suitors, but our primary emotion was annoyance, as with the lads messing about, we were late for our end-of-holiday disco! I thought Dom looked great in his ski gear and he was a really proficient skier from day one, but I still didn't get together with him on this holiday, instead I ended up kissing a boy called Will at the disco, who was from a grammar school somewhere down south.

~

In our final and sixth year we sat our O levels and it must have been a long hot summer, as I remember a small group of girls gathering together at each other's houses and sitting in our gardens whilst revising and catching some rays. When it was time for them to come to my house to revise, we were distracted by some young Libyan students, who were renting the house next door for a short time. They always came into the garden with their prayer mats in tow and faced Mecca, whilst praying.

This particular day, they had their chart music blaring out of the house. Instead of asking them to turn it down, we went in direct competition with them and would turn our music up more to drown out theirs. This went on for quite a while.

When we went around to another girl's house, we used to play UB40 videos over and over, and ogle Ali Campbell. There was a song 'Don't Break my Heart' that UB40 had released and in the video there was a scene where the whole video paused until Ali Campbell did a cheeky nudge of the radio and then it started again. We all fancied him and played it over and over again, fast-forwarding and rewinding it accordingly! It really was a miracle that we actually all got good marks in the end!

College

I don't think my teenage years were that rebellious; however, I can recall two incidents that could be classified as such, within the parameters of our strict Catholic upbringing.

The first was when we were playing outside our new house in Bryone Drive. One of Andrew's friends had upset me and I was standing outside our garage door, one of those retractable ones on rollers, and I said a swear word back at David. Within a flash the garage door slid open and Dad shouted:

"Jane, I think you had better come inside right now."

It just wasn't appropriate to use those words, especially within earshot of your parents, and I knew better.

The other incident was when at the age of seventeen, and after embarking on my first serious relationship, I made an appointment with my family doctor, marched in and asked to go on the mini-pill (unlike some of my close friends who all went to family planning clinics on the other side of Manchester, using false names!). Afterwards I told my mum what I had done. I was young and very naïve, but in my mind

JANE COUPES

I just felt that I had to be responsible for my own actions throughout any relationship.

Life continued in the normal vein for me and I went on to sixth form college at Xaverian College in Rusholme, partly due to my chosen subjects, particularly as I had wanted to do business studies, partly when I found out that the ratio of boys to girls was three to one! In reality, I ended up studying English literature, economics and social and economic history at A level and resitting my maths O level. I was still struggling with my maths O level work, so the lecturer, Mr Holt, gave me extra help at lunchtimes. As I was allowed to wander into the staffroom to see him, there was a rumour going around the college that I was having an affair with him! Nothing could have been further from the truth as, although he has a really nice bloke, he was old enough to be my dad!

I left early, before actually sitting my A levels, to embark on a career in banking. I had applied to all the major banks and attended interviews (Mum and Dad bought me a beautiful black suit size eight from Planet for my interviews!) with Barclays and Allied Irish Bank. I had to complete psychometric tests held at Manchester University for the Allied Irish job then I was told that I was unsuccessful, but could ring for feedback. After I had started working at Barclays, Allied Irish rang me and offered me a job, but I decided to stick with Barclays, as by now I had settled quite well.

I started as a junior in June 1986 for Barclays Bank PLC and gradually worked my way up, covering lots of roles in the meantime. I started doing junior, cashiering, book-keeping in the back room, processing cheques, dealing with general queries etc.

I then decided to have a complete change and covered a role as a secretary, whilst also doing typing at night school. I moved location on numerous occasions and out of Manchester for the first time, and worked as a secretary/PA-type role for one of the managers at Wilmslow Branch. This was a real culture shock for me; instead of going to the pub at lunchtimes, my colleagues at Wilmslow mostly used to go home and walk the dog or hang washing out. It was bizarre after Manchester, and I found a few of the customers to be rude and arrogant.

One of my colleagues had always worked in Manchester until now, like me, and she joked and said:

"I'd rather go back to Manchester and deal with the tramps."

They used to walk in and steal all the stationery!

At this time Barclays introduced internal job advertising and as I had already expressed an interest in personnel (and was doing a business course at night school specialising in human resources) I applied for a job as a secretary in personnel at the local head office in Manchester. I was successful and enjoyed the change of scene. It was nice to get away from angry customers and just deal with staff, potential recruits and visitors from other corporate companies.

~

In a parallel universe, Dom was busy travelling the world. He took a year out from his studies at Manchester University, where he was doing business studies, and spent a year in Australia. We continued to write to each other even though by now I had embarked on my first serious relationship with a boy I had met whilst working at my first ever Saturday job.

At the age of sixteen I took a Saturday job at a local shop on the A6 near Stepping Hill Hospital. The shop was split into two halves. One half of the unit was a fresh flower shop and

I learned about flower arranging etc., and the other half was a fruit and vegetable shop where I got used to dealing with the general public at large. I worked there with a girl called Sharon, whom I had known from Brownies a long time before. She had gone to the local Great Moor Primary School, like lots of my friends who were neighbours. She was really friendly with a boy called Conrad and he would call into the shop every Saturday on his way to watch Manchester City play at Maine Road. He liked the look of me, and vice versa, and within a couple of months we were an item.

I would best describe this relationship by using a quote from a Kirsty MacColl song. The line went, 'I put you on a pedestal; you put me on the pill.' I was a bad judge of character and, although I had some fun, this relationship ended after five years.

Before Dominic had gone off to Australia, Conrad and I, plus Dom and all his friends, used to frequent the same pub in Hazel Grove, The George & Dragon. Even though I mixed with both sets of friends in there, Conrad always said to me that Dominic and I got on a bit too well for his liking! Whilst Dominic went off on his travels, Conrad went to Liverpool University to study genetics.

When I finished work on a Friday afternoon, I would often get the train or drive my first ever car over to Liverpool and stay there for the weekend, either with Conrad in his student digs or my old school friend, Tanya, who was also in Liverpool studying business studies at Liverpool Polytechnic. I had some fantastic weekends over in Liverpool city centre and we had regular bars/clubs to which we used to go.

I was in this relationship from 1985 until 1991 when we split up as he was having an affair with his boss. I was completely devastated and after I eventually got over it I wrote to Dom in one of our regular letters, *by the way, I've split with Conrad.*

When Dominic returned from his travels, he had a great tan and looked very handsome. We continued to socialise in the same circle of friends until I discovered that he liked me, and after a conversation with his cousin, Maria, and checking I was on to a sure thing, I asked him out for lunch. In my previous relationship I had thought Conrad was 'the one'. Very quickly as Dominic and I started dating, I realised that this had not been the case and I had now found 'the one'. We started seeing more and more of each other, even though Dominic was studying hard for his accountancy qualifications and was even sacrificing his Saturday football games to sit vital exams in Manchester!

After that we became an item and I guess the rest is history.

~

The terrible stomach pains after I ate continued and, as far as my health goes, by the age of seventeen I had already been subjected to hospital tests that usually only older people have. As a result of lots of investigations to enable the doctors to diagnose me, I had already experienced the delights of a colonoscopy, gastroscopy and a barium meal! These investigations had come about after me having to go and see a psychologist.

My dad used to pick me up from work during both our lunch hours once a week and we would drive to Withington Hospital to see the doctor. I remember his first name was Digby and he seemed quite strange, and he used to ask me lots of very personal questions. The doctors had told my mum and dad that they thought I was anorexic and that was why I was losing weight. I knew that this was not the case, so had agreed to see this doctor. He would weigh me every week and he asked me to keep a diary of what I was eating. I did so and he kept on saying:

"This looks like quite a healthy diet, it seems really strange that you are not putting on weight."

This went on week after week until he said it again and I challenged him.

"Are you calling me a liar?"

In what seemed like no time at all he had referred me to a female colleague of his who specialised in gastrology, and this was when all the tests were lined up and I was diagnosed with Crohn's disease.

~

At seventeen, I was one of those people who was itching to drive. I signed up for lessons shortly after my seventeenth birthday and, therefore, after about twenty lessons, coupled with Dad's tuition (when we went out practising and came back not speaking!), I passed my driving test first time and was totally thrilled that I had a new level of independence. As part of my instruction, Dad used to give me extra lessons during the morning rush hour into Manchester. I found it stressful, but it was definitely the best 'hands on' experience. I would drive his blue Ford Orion into Manchester, where I would get out and then Dad took his car to work and I would get the train to Ashburys Station after work and meet him for my lift home.

My first ever car I bought was a maroon Fiesta, registration number B332 SNA. The second car I bought was a gleaming, flame red, brand new Ford Fiesta, registration number G348 WVM. It was my pride and joy to drive it. At that time we had three cars in our family; my dad's, Andrew's and mine. One was parked in the garage, one on the drive and one on the road outside the house.

On a cold October night having arrived home from work, I parked my new vehicle on the road ready to go to college after a quick change and some tea. My car was only a few weeks old, so I parked it very carefully. Our drive was directly in line with the house across the road and my car was situated so they could get on and off their drive easily. Our neighbour, Barry, who lived in the house opposite, was an experienced police driver and had given me many tips whilst I had been learning to drive a few years earlier.

Putting on my coat at around ten past seven there was an almighty crash, and a car alarm started screeching away. Opening the door to go outside, I felt the need to use Victor Meldrew's catchphrase:

"I don't believe it!"

Barry's car was embedded into my driver's side front wing! There were floods of tears and as Barry and my dad tried to comfort me, Barry said how annoyed he was with himself and also he had ignored one of the very first tips he had given me, which was, 'Whichever direction you are going it helps to see that everything is clear'! The car was repaired in the Ford dealers and it came back like a brand new one again and gave me many years of enjoyment, but what a catastrophe!

~

On the very first evening when I started my business course at Davenport College at night school, I met my friend, Julia. We hit it off immediately and had a very similar sense of humour. The second week of our course we decided to go out afterwards to a local nightclub (on a Monday night!) and whilst in there we discovered that we had some mutual friends. We bumped into my old girlfriends whom I had known since being very young when we had all lived in Coombes Street, and I then discovered that they all knew Julia's current boyfriend and were all friendly.

I soon became a member of this group and we went out and partied most nights, especially at weekends, dancing the nights away. Our regular haunt was Quaffers and even though we tried lots of different venues, most of the time we ended up getting a taxi back there, as by now we knew lots of the regulars. Our group of friends were every taxi driver's worst nightmare. The band, Showaddywaddy's 'Under the Moon of Love' hit was always our chosen song to shrill in drunken voices whilst being transported from various drinking haunts in Stockport to Quaffers, where we were all gold members and had cards to prove it!

Dominic also started going in there with some of his football buddies and after our lunch out, we stuck to going out with our own friends every Friday and would then meet up at the end of the evening.

A Bundle of Pink

Dominic and I were married at St Mary's RC Church in Marple Bridge on Saturday, 9th November, 1996. They say it is lucky to have rain on your wedding day; well, we had heaps before and during our ceremony. Afterwards it brightened up and transformed into a crisp autumn day. Our reception was at The Hunting Lodge, Adlington Hall in the Cheshire countryside and we had a large reception with lots of our old school friends and family.

In the evening more friends, work colleagues and Dom's football friends came to join in our celebrations. It was a very special day and I know this sounds really clichéd, but we could feel the love and support around us as we embarked on our life together. We even commented afterwards that we were really lucky to have both sets of parents there, especially as our mums and dads get on really well with each other. That felt quite rare, as we had friends whose parents were no longer around or had split up, and we also commented on that. However, because we both had large families and a huge circle of friends, that meant there had been a few argumentative words over the table arrangements at our sit-down meal.

During my dad's speech he told several stories about me during my childhood. However, he told one in particular about how I got him into trouble before I was even born! Basically, my mum was very big when she carried me and she had been having labour pains all throughout the night. She had delivered my brother very quickly, so had been warned not to hang around with this baby. They went to drop Andrew off with our neighbour in Coombes Street at that time, Mrs Farmer, and then went onwards to the hospital. As they arrived, the evening shift had just finished and the morning staff had just arrived to start their shift at 7.30 a.m. Dad was greeted by a battleaxe of a nurse, who folded her arms and said to him:

"Have you booked her in, because this process can take up to seven minutes, you know?"

Dad went to do so and when he came back, said he was bombarded with:

"Do you know we've had to take her to theatre? Do you know that we've had no time to prepare her? Do you know that it costs four times as much if you come in at the last minute?"

Dad thinks she smiled for a second and then said:

"Do you know you've had a baby girl?"

He had missed the main event, as I had been in such a hurry to be born, and he had been told off at the same time!

One other thing that Dad said in his speech that has stuck with me was when he commented on how he had been gob-smacked when I walked down the stairs in my wedding dress. He went on to say:

"Underneath this beautiful dress is quite a tough young lady."

Your parents know you really well and, of course, Dad had already identified this feisty or quietly determined attribute of mine before I had embarked on my married life. Since being ill, it has made me wonder, did someone somewhere know that I potentially had the capacity and tenacity to cope relatively well with the deal I had been given?

Our wedding day

Before our wedding day, we had started to put down some roots and had bought a house on Kayswood Road in Marple, near Rose Hill train station. Looking back, those were halcyon days, as both our careers were progressing well (I had now taken up a position as personnel assistant in Barclays Manchester head office and Dom was now fully qualified and

JANE COUPES

working his way up the ladder with Ernst & Young). We had a house that we were desperately trying to make our mark on, we had endless holidays, meals out and weekends away to see friends who were dotted around the country.

Under no illusions that we had the most perfect marriage, I just feel it is relevant to mention that in the pre-child years we had only three arguments of note and these were about totally trivial things, and were resolved very quickly.

The first one was shortly after our wedding and was when Dom left his football kit in his football bag rather than transferring it to the washing basket one Sunday. By the next Sunday he wondered why the washing fairies hadn't read his mind and laundered it. Instead there was a sweaty smell in the hall where I felt it had gone rancid. Needless to say, after I shouted at him he never did it again!

Our second argument was over a Chinese meal. Dom is renowned within our peer group for his extremely large appetite and we were sharing a starter in our favourite Chinese restaurant at that time in High Lane. Crispy aromatic duck is one of my favourite dishes too and we had a row over who was having the last pancake. We did actually share it in the end, but I was cross that he had presumed that he had a divine right to it because I had a smaller appetite!

The last argument of note was when we were dealing with some paperwork and bills. As an accountant, Dom has always taken control of managing our joint finances and I have always dealt with all the paperwork aspect. On this occasion, I didn't feel he was including me in decisions, so we had words and I got so cross I threw the hole-punch at him!

I have always had quite bad PMT and Dom has always joked and said once a month he should lock me in a room by myself for a week. This PMT usually played a big part in our cross words. The rest of the time we were both very non-con-frontational. I once read a magazine article where they analysed which star signs were compatible and for ours (Capricorn and Virgo) it said, 'Still waters run deep', and that quote has stayed with me ever since. I can be the fiery one when tested and his calming, laid-back influence usually means we are very compatible.

So with everything going well, when is the right time to have our first child? A family had always been on the cards for Dominic and me, assuming that we could have children, of course. We didn't presume, and planned the right time for us to have a child. Once we were reassured it was a good time with regards to my health and our finances, we threw caution to the wind, stopped taking precautions and on a holiday to Sorrento conceived Emily.

When I worked back my dates and discovered that she had been conceived in Sorrento, I joked with my work colleagues. At this time because of a very high profile celebrity couple, it was quite trendy to name your child after the place where they were conceived. I joked to our small team in personnel saying the baby may well be called Vesuvius Coupes! If you have ever visited Sorrento, you will know that Naples Bay is overshadowed by Mount Vesuvius! In truth, we named her 'Emily Jane' as we both really liked these two names together. On a visit to see Dom's Nana Vi, who was very elderly and resident in a nursing home in Sale back then, she told us that her own mother's name had been 'Emily Gertrude'!

Dom didn't even know that Emily was in fact already a family name and that just made it perfect for our little angel. However, although we adopted the name Emily, we left the name Gertrude firmly etched in history! Sadly, although

Nana Vi was around at the time of Emily's arrival, her health deteriorated and she died shortly afterwards.

My employers were flexible with all the time off for doctors' appointments and ante-natal checks etc. It was very exciting as a first-time mum to feel my baby growing inside me and follow each stage in full, enhanced with my guidebook, *Emma's Diary*. This was the book that my midwife gave me and it proved avid reading on the train to and from work. When I felt the bubbles in my stomach that were her first kicks and when I got the opportunity to listen to my baby's heartbeat at ante-natal checks with the midwife they were really exciting and awe-inspiring events.

My hormones were all over the show. During a conversation with my friend, Michelle, who was also pregnant with her first child, we both admitted to walking into a Mothercare store and hardly believing that soon some of the baby equipment and paraphernalia would be in situ in our homes. It made us quite tearful and gave that goosebump effect.

There were quite a few others in our circle of friends who were having this adventure at the same time. I especially spent lots of time with our friend, Jane, whose due date was four months before mine, more or less exactly the same time as Michelle's. After work Jane and I would meet up in Manchester and get the train back to Stockport Swimming Pool, where we swam up to 30 lengths and then sat in the jacuzzi comparing pregnancy notes! Jane, Michelle and I got together quite a lot during our respective maternity leave periods. Some of our other friends were already on their second child and considered experts, so we all pooled our resources and experiences, and joked about the extreme ways in which our lives had and were about to change.

~

At Emily's birth, my community midwife, Anne, had said that she had really enjoyed it because Dom and I were bantering in the delivery suite. When my waters broke, I said to him:

"Has it gone everywhere?"

"It's like something out of the *X Files*. Didn't you see it hit the back wall over there just then?" he replied.

When I was pushing he kept urging me to 'come on' in a football chanting style, which he had threatened to do beforehand, and I had told him not to because he would make me laugh! When Emily's head started to come he kept on telling me that the baby had ginger hair.

I know Anne particularly enjoyed sharing our packet of Maynards wine gums that Dom had brought along to keep our strength up during the birth, as she commented that wine gums should be essential kit for all couples and nursing staff!

"We have a couple of student midwives on secondment at the moment. Do you mind if they come in to watch your baby being delivered?" Anne asked, just as Emily's head was coming through.

Anyone who knows me will know that I have never really liked being the centre of attention, so Dom and I were both really shocked when I casually said:

"Yeah, just bring them all in!"

Some women talk about the birth of their children being so emotional that their partners cry. Dom did not cry at Emily's birth, but after I had been in hospital for three nights with Emily and he could see how tired I was, we sat down and both cried together. The realisation had hit us; now we were both supposed to look after this little girl and had been entrusted with her upbringing. We felt very responsible all of a sudden.

"We've created a monster!" I said.

Emily was, nevertheless, a perfect and angelic monster, on whom we both doted!

~

I was actually really fortunate that whilst carrying Emily, thinking ahead already to my return to work, I was quickly promoted to the next grade up and made a team leader of our section. I had applied once for the team leader job, but had not been successful at interview; however, I received feedback, took it all on board, and worked on some flaws and my interview technique. Being pregnant also took some of the pressure off and next time I was rewarded with a favourable outcome.

This decision involved our first ever row after having Emily, when Dom had said he wasn't really comfortable with my decision to return to work and especially with me taking on extra responsibilities. We had a row and I told him his views were very old-fashioned and that he was a caveman!

In actual fact, right from the outset, Dom was a very 'hands on' dad. He is the eldest of four children, so was very comfortable handling Emily and helping me with every aspect of her care when work commitments allowed him to be around.

After having Emily I had experienced an awful time in hospital. We had paid to have a private room, as I was a first-time mum and wanted to get to grips with feeding/changing etc., in private. At night-time Emily had been very hungry and it seemed that I had to constantly breastfeed her. At the time I felt very vulnerable and I can remember feeling that the nursing staff didn't seem particularly interested or want to help me to settle her. In fact, one of the night staff had stomped down to my room when I buzzed, and she actually squeezed my nipple saying:

"Let's see if you have actually got any milk coming through!"

I felt violated, but was so vulnerable that I never said anything at the time.

I initially struggled with feeding Emily. It was a little bit sore at first, but once she latched on, the toe curling stopped and she fed well. However, she also fed in small amounts very frequently, so I struggled to keep up the milk supply and also was so tired, as all I seemed to do was feed her. I saw some fantastic sunrises as 4 a.m., which seemed to frequently be her favourite waking time!

I can honestly say that the birth bit had been easy and quick for me, except for when her head came through and Anne, my midwife, said:

"This bit will feel like it is burning now."

She was right and it really did burn, but then Emily's head came right out and the rest of her followed really quickly. However, the aspect of motherhood I was not prepared for was that thereafter every time I tried to have a meal or take a shower, there was a little person demanding to be fed!

The week after Emily was born, my dad had just retired and he often used to call around to mow our grass or tend the garden, and he would often look after Emily at the same time, so that I could actually get a shower in peace. Dom took charge at mealtimes and was fantastic in taking over so that I could actually eat a healthy meal, to help keep my strength up for constant and continual feeding.

After endless desperate calls to Dom at work for the first

eight weeks, I was on the verge of giving up breastfeeding and when I told my health visitor this she advised me to do alternate feeds with breast and bottle, thereby slowly introducing a formula bottle. This I did, and continued to breastfeed Emily until she was nine months old and she nipped me with one of her first teeth. Definitely time to give up then!

I had taken extended maternity leave and it was coming to the time when I was due to return to work, therefore, childcare needed to be sorted out, so that I would be happy with my decision to return to work part-time. Both our mums were busy with work/retirement, so we explored other avenues. My brother and cousin and their wives recommended a private nursery in Davenport to which they had both sent their children, so with two family recommendations and two of my friends working there, one as a nursery nurse and the other managing the nursery for the owner, the decision was made.

We went to have a tour around the nursery, but this was just a formality and to show Dom what it was like. In my mind it was a done deal and the only way I would be happy to leave Emily and continue my career. It would cost us, but it would be worth it. I negotiated working Thursdays and Fridays to begin with, so I would still get three days at home with Emily to spend some quality time with her. I never minded working the end of the week, as it was easier to get those set days at the nursery, also my colleagues in the office were chirpier towards the end of the week and it also meant I didn't miss out on the Friday lunchtimes in the pub for lunch and a quick drink!

Emily & Daniel's school photo - 2007

~

Before she started nursery Emily had a trial run and this involved me dropping her off and leaving her properly for the first time ever. I was to leave her for a few hours over the lunchtime period, so I decided to go and do some shopping, which I thought would distract me from any negative thoughts about leaving her. This did work to a degree and I went over to M & S at Handforth Dean and did some shopping. However, as I did not have Emily and a pram with me, I was finished in record time and felt a bit strange and empty. When I told Dom later I said that not having Emily with me felt like losing my right arm. If I had actually known at that time what it was like to be without the use of an arm, maybe I would have chosen my words differently!

Emily settled into nursery really well and after that initial wrench when I dropped her off every morning I went to Davenport Station to catch the train into Manchester and continue my career. It didn't help when the night before I was due to return to work, I watched a documentary on television, which stated that children who stay at home with their mothers during the early years do better when they enter a school environment! Not at all what I wanted to hear now I had made my decision and was happy that the combination of some of my quality time and a structured nursery regime would make her the very independent, but the quietly confident and bright child she is today.

PART THREE
REHABILITATION

Over The Wall

So, back to my treatment, post stroke in hospital...

The heart drugs were working wonders, so I was soon transferred to a more general ward, A11. I continued with the heart drugs then they put me on even more drugs to prevent another blood clot occurring. These were heparin (which has to be injected into your stomach!), aspirin and also Warfarin, the blood thinning drug usually associated with elderly patients. As I was taking Warfarin, I had to have blood taken every single day to check my INR (International Nutrition Ratio) level, and this then determined what dosage of the drug I required. As my blood was being taken so regularly, the veins in my arm would blow and I was really badly bruised, as the nursing staff had difficulty finding a spot where my weedy arms had not already been stabbed!

I have lots of memories when I was transferred to ward A11 in the hospital. This was because I was getting slightly better all the time. I will stick to the most prominent memories rather than completely bore you. I started to learn more about strokes on this ward and the way in which it had affected me, but also some of the things that I had luckily escaped - like losing your speech completely and losing the ability to swallow or even breathe. One of the occupational therapists gave me a printed leaflet about the effects of stroke and I learned there was now a question of my ability to drive or even walk.

I had just been reading one of these leaflets when Dr Lewis came to do his weekly ward rounds. He said that now the nurses were to arrange for me to have regular physiotherapy and occupational therapy, and to give me the complete works. He joked with the staff and said they were to treat me as if I was in training for the Olympic Games. I remember joking also and saying that I would now technically be eligible to compete in the Para-Olympics!

As an aside, I now need to tell you that just a week or so before I delivered Daniel, we had bought a new car for me. At the time Dom's company car was a Volkswagen Golf GTI and as I was on the insurance, I loved driving it and picking up my girlfriends. I had always wanted a Golf of my own, but we had waited until we could justify needing a five-door car. My new Golf was a reliable solid German car to transport the children around in. It was a 'V' registration, which was virtually new at the time, jazz blue in colour and I immediately loved it.

One day Dom came to visit me in the hospital.

"I've got something important that I need to ask you. What do you think we should do about your car?" he asked.

He then went on to tell me that as I could no longer drive, it seemed a waste to just keep the car and have it sitting on the drive at home. He told me he had made enquiries at the local dealership and they had said that under the circumstances there was a possibility that they would buy it back from us and give us the full price. He asked me what my thoughts were.

"I will be 'Mrs Gutted from Stockport', but I think we should get them to take it back."

This seemed like the best idea, especially as we had taken out a loan to buy the car.

"I'm glad that is what you think, because they came to pick it up this morning!" Dom said, turning around to face me.

He had made the decision without me anyway. I remember swearing at this confession and feeling that this stroke really was going to drastically alter my lifestyle. I had only driven my brand new car three times and now it was going back to the garage. He then said that when I was able to drive again he would get me another Golf, but next time a better specification with any adaptations that were needed.

My friend, Michelle, also came to visit me on the ward. She had delivered twins girls exactly six weeks before I had Daniel, so she was telling me how she was getting on. She also has a little boy, Alex, who is four months older than Emily. I tried to join in the conversation, but was just so poorly that I kept closing my eyes to rest them. For a long time I felt bad that I was not more sociable when she had taken the time and effort to come and see me when she probably had better things to do.

~

The physiotherapy I received was very gentle to begin with and it was really quite a clever method that they used to start to get me on my way back to full fitness. However, I only realised what they were doing a long time after the event. While it was taking place I just wanted to get back into bed and sleep forever. I did not want to get out of bed and sit in a chair and read my *Hello* magazine for half an hour and gradually build the time up!

~

It was Mother's Day while I was on this ward. Dom went to a lot of trouble and bought me some lovely cards from himself and the children. They had nice words in them to say what a good mummy I was and how I made our home a nice place to be. Of course I filled up immediately. He had also bought me some perfume from Emily, a whole bottle of Oscar De La Renta, my new favourite perfume! Daniel had bought me some chenille bedsocks and a new portable compact disc player. I was very touched, but really all I wanted was to be at home with my children on Mother's Day.

I remember thinking about all my friends who would be waking up with their children and opening their presents with them in bed. I felt that I was really missing out. As I lay on that bed on A11, this was the first opportunity that I was well enough to reflect on how I had ended up there and I really struggled to comprehend why things had gone so horribly wrong.

Now I was on a more general ward I was subjected to other patients and their moans and groans. I felt very sorry for some of the ladies on my ward who were very poorly, but that did not stop me feeling irritated when they would not be quiet and would endlessly shout for the nurses' attention.

One afternoon, Dominic's cousin, Philip, and his wife, Tracy, came to visit me. They live in Nottingham, so I was very pleased they had travelled to see me. While they were still visiting and we were chatting they were also subjected to the other ladies' moans and groans. Philip asked me how I coped with it, and I was brutally honest and said that it was really getting on my nerves and stopping me sleeping at night sometimes. He then went on to tell me that he had a tiny radio with headphones in his pocket that he used to listen to results at football matches. I could borrow it to try and help the situation. That night I was able to drown out all the noise on the ward and I had a well-needed good night's sleep!

I could still remember most words and was able to speak to my visitors or 'guests' as I sometimes incorrectly called them. My speech was very slurred and I think I sounded as though I had been drinking alcohol. If only that had been the case! Even though I could still recall words and their correct meanings, my voice had become quieter and there was no inflection or tone in my speech. I sounded like a robot. I also learned that I now had a crooked smile, with the left side of my face drooping, as my cheek muscles were now weak and slightly paralysed. The speech therapist gave me some exercises that I had to practise daily, which involved me looking stupid whilst saying the sounds 'ooh' and 'aah' in a pronounced way and trying to get my cheek muscles working again.

Four of my girlfriends, with whom I often used to get together, arranged to come and visit me in hospital. It was nice to catch up on all their gossip and find out what was happening in the real world. Two of them, who just happen to be sisters, Debi and Lisa, told me that they had both been busy booking their wedding venues for later that year. Debi and Owen had chosen to go to Las Vegas in the May, and Lisa and Lee were to be married in Cyprus in October. They both went on to tell me that when they came back they planned to have evening receptions in our local area to celebrate their marriages. I remember telling them that I would be present at both of them. Deep down I had reservations, but knew in my heart that I really wanted to go. I just could not see that far ahead in my life and what state I would be in. I realised that I had said I would be there with a fighting spirit that I did not truly feel yet!

Whilst on Ward A11, I started to get cramp in my left toes. This was complete agony and sometimes prevented me from sleeping properly. I was told that this cramp was a good thing and could be the start of my feeling coming back. However, at the time I felt cross that I was in a hospital and nobody could help with simple cramps. My dad, who had retired around the time I had Emily, if you remember, used to come to the hospital in the mornings and massage my feet with baby lotion. I even remember one of the old ladies on the ward rubbing my foot one night when I could not sleep!

Another of the old ladies engaged all the patients in a long tale about a love affair that she had had with an American GI during one of the world wars. These two old ladies used to threaten to do waltzes and sambas up and down the ward, and I would goad them on. They were thrilled when my mother and father-in-law brought me a CD player to have in hospital. I remember listening to it with my headphones on and Nora asked me what I was listening to. When I told her it was the theme music from *Titanic*, she asked if they could all listen too and the staff nurse who was on duty that day turned the volume right up and took my headphones off, so that the whole ward was flooded with eerie Irish music.

I was hoping they would kick me out and send me home, but it never happened. It was just a relief I wasn't listening to some of the other CDs in my collection.

Another day when the physiotherapists came to work with me they asked what I wanted to do.

"Can we try some walking?" I asked.

The girls were great, and I looked forward to the sessions very much, not only for the physiotherapy, but also their young conversation cheered me up. Anyway, they decided that as I was feeling brave we would go for it. I had already advanced to being able to do what they call 'transfer'. This means that you can manoeuvre yourself out of your wheelchair and into another chair by standing, turning and holding your own weight in the middle. This was a really big step forwards and meant I was getting stronger.

I put my slippers on for the first time in ages and placed my feet on the floor. The physiotherapists then assisted me. Beth put her arm around my shoulders and Laura looked after my knees to make sure they didn't buckle beneath me. She then helped me to move my feet one in front of the other. We kept on going. It felt so good to be upright after all this time that we continued until I had nearly walked the full length of the ward. Fantastic! My fellow patients said I was doing really well and they cheered me on.

When Dom came to visit that night I could not wait to tell him. I stood up and gave him a big hug, an upright hug - another big step. This also felt really good and later when we started chatting I was all fired up and told him that the race was on. Who would learn to walk first - Mummy or Daniel?

~

"This seminar could be really positive for your recovery," said Beth, my physio, whilst visiting me on A11.

So that is how I found myself standing in the hospital gym in my pyjamas, surrounded by around twenty physiotherapists, all dressed in their white and navy uniforms.

I had been instructed to wear my little short pyjamas, so that they could all see my torso closely and all my muscles as

I slowly attempted to move. A top physio from Macclesfield Hospital had been invited to teach a group of physios her new pioneering techniques and I was to be the model on whom she was working.

It was quite daunting, but I also thought that she might observe something crucial to my recovery, and indeed she made a discovery that my right side was heavily over-compensating for my left side, but it was so secretive and crafty that there was no evidence of this when watching my body and its patterns of movement.

～

Ward A11 was split into two parts by a wall that actually finished about a foot from the ceiling. Dom had now started to stagger his return to work and was going in to the office when he could (subject to babysitters for the children) and also working from home.

One day he came to visit me on his way to work. He was dressed in his suit and one of the ladies from the other side of the partition said:

"Here's that lovely, good-looking young doctor."

"No, he's not a doctor, he belongs to that young woman in the corner with the baby!" another lady said.

Another time a little old lady came to apologise to Dom that she could not give him her urine sample until she had taken another drink with her dinner!

The daughter of one of Dom's mum's friends was on the other side of the ward. She was a young girl called Gemma, who had just been diagnosed with probable Crohn's disease. We became friends because of this common condition and also because we were the only two patients on the ward who were aged this side of sixty. We used to moan to each other about being stuck in hospital and all the things we were miss-ing in the outside world. Gemma was a student studying hairdressing and beauty at Buxton College. We supported each other emotionally after two of the old ladies on the ward collapsed, died, the curtains were drawn around their beds, their families were brought in to be advised of the news and finally the bodies were carried out.

The experts said that I had to wait for an assessment to see if it was appropriate for me to be transferred to Cherry Tree, a nearby unit set up purely for people with neurological conditions. I remember Dr Downton's SHO came to assess me. He asked me lots of clever questions to test my cognitive thinking and then he asked me to repeat sequences of num-bers back to him (a breeze for someone who had previously worked in a bank, having to remember account details etc). The difficult bit for me was when he started to place objects in the palm of my hand and ask me what they were. I specifi-cally remember feeling an item that felt like it was spherical with ridges on it, like a nut of some sort. Later when I asked the doctor what it was, he told me that it was a two pence piece, totally flat only with very fine ridges of pattern on it! This was the first time I realised that I had sensory problems on top of everything else.

The doctor also brought along a three-dimensional model of the brain, and he pointed to it and showed me the area that the CT scan had shown was affected in my case. It was quite a large portion of the top of my head and obviously the section that controls the left side of the body, now no longer working for me.

There was some good news, as I was soon to be transferred to Cherry Tree. Here they were specially geared up for pa-tients with strokes and neurological problems. I learned that my physiotherapy and occupational therapies were soon to become very intense, and I could spend anything from six months to two years there. I saw this as a new challenge and could not wait to get there, especially as at Cherry Tree Hospital you were allowed to go home every single weekend to see your family! Also Cherry Tree was geographically closer to our new house in Offerton, so I felt I was getting closer to my ultimate dream of going home.

Before I found out my date to be transferred across to the other hospital, Dr Lewis arranged with the nurses that I could have an afternoon home visit. I remember borrowing a red wheelchair from the hospital and going home for a Sunday afternoon. It felt wonderful to be home with my family, and I realised that I had missed my home comforts and family very much.

~

I was transferred to Cherry Tree Hospital on 1st April, 2001, yes April Fool's Day. When I arrived in a wheelchair taxi, I was admitted to the Devonshire Centre there, which was for younger people with head injuries. This was a brand new hospital building built on the site next to the field where I used to play as a child, so quite near Mum and Dad's house. So, this is what was over the wall where I used to climb, but never ventured over!

Here I soon came to learn an awful lot about head injuries and what they can do to you. There were patients there of all ages and from all kinds of backgrounds, and they were all at different stages of their recovery. I quickly got to know some of the patients and became friendly with the ones who were well enough to talk. I remember a man called Harry, who became a bit of an inspiration to me. He was quite far on in his recovery compared to me and, although I never found out what happened to him, I could not believe how cheerful he was all the time. He was a real character and a bit of a tonic to have around the hospital. He liked to bet on horse races and encouraged us all to study the runners and riders with him over breakfast.

The hospital routine here was very structured and encouraged you to look after yourself as much as you could, within your limits. In the reception area there was a huge whiteboard with all the patients' names on it. It was split into a timetable with different therapies, including occupational therapy, physiotherapy, psychotherapy and to my delight, aromatherapy! I quickly learned that you were to get washed and dressed by yourself and were to be ready for your therapy times. Visitors were allowed to call any time except when you were in therapies. You were expected to go to the dining room at mealtimes and the rest of the time was free time. Dr Downton, a top female neurological consultant, ran this regime, and at this point Dr Lewis transferred my care to her.

Dr Downton had already said that because I had two small children to look after in the real world, I needed to be very fit and well when I was eventually discharged, so this may involve me staying there longer than the average person.

My time in Cherry Tree was very eventful. It was like living on the set of a soap opera. I will just share with you the major storylines or ones that are most relevant to me.

I was shown around the purpose-built building and I thought that I would never remember where all the different rooms were. For the first couple of days I thought that there were two storeys, with the ward and patients' rooms on the first floor, and all the therapy rooms and gym on the ground. In fact, the whole building was single storey built in an 'L' shape and, of course, there were no stairs to tackle in a neurological hospital where most of the patients struggled to walk!

One of my earliest memories in Cherry Tree was a few mornings after I had arrived. I had been admitted to a small ward with four beds in it near the nurses' station. I was told that they would observe me and as I got better I might be moved to a double room, or even have a room of my own, depending on my progress.

This particular morning I remember feeling tired because of all the upheaval of moving hospitals, and the other patients were just starting to awaken when a nurse burst through the doors of the ward. She began to sing a Nelly Furtado song that was in the charts at the time.

"I'm like a bird, I'll only fly away."

This was at 7 a.m. in the morning! I don't know what she put in her tea, but she was always like this; a very hyper bubbly personality. She later brought in her holiday pictures to show us, as she had just come back from a girls' holiday in Barbados. I immediately took a shine to her and I later found out that she was called Brenda.

I gradually became alert enough to read a book and concentrate during this time. The book was called *After Stroke* and had been written by a man called David Hinds. He had suffered a stroke when he was in his forties. I really identified with a lot of the things he was saying in his book. One thing that puzzled me was that he wrote a whole chapter on depression. At that early stage of my recovery, it was the one area where I totally did not relate to David. I thought it just would not happen to me. I would just deal with it and move on.

When I looked around at the other patients on the ward,

there was a lady who looked about the same age as me, maybe a bit younger, and two older ladies. It struck me as being very strange that they all had cot sides up on both sides of their beds to stop them falling out. I associated this precaution with children of Emily's age and was a little confused as to why they were required.

The ward made a very good vantage point for watching everybody's visitors arriving. One day the distinctive noise of the door buzzer sounded and I looked up to see if the visitors were for me. They were two young ladies whom I did not recognize, then I saw one of the nurses on duty point to me through the window. As the two ladies walked towards me, I started to recognise them. They were Sharon and Sharan, the two young nurses who had become friends when I was on the coronary care unit in Stepping Hill Hospital. I had not recognised them, as they were both in casual clothes and not uniform. They were both having some study time off before their exams commenced. It was lovely to see them both again and I thought it was really kind of them to take the trouble to come and see me. We had a good chat and then I wished them good luck for their exams. They had said that I looked really well, so that was a big confidence boost to me.

Soon after I settled into the new routine of the hospital, I realised that I was going through the 'why did this happen to me?' phase of my recovery. Dom helped me through this by telling me to look around at my fellow patients. It was obvious that some of them would never go home and be able to look after themselves.

"At least you will be coming home. It might take a long time, but it will happen," he said, encouragingly.

He also tried to say to me that we were in fact lucky; we had two stunningly beautiful children, a nice house and each other. At the time we had friends who could not conceive children or had lost babies. We were very lucky in that both times when we wanted children, we had conceived almost straightaway. In fact, we used to joke and say Dom only had to look at me in a certain way and I became pregnant!

I knew that in the past I could be stroppy with the best of them.

"Am I really such a horrible person that I deserve all this?" I asked my husband.

"Of course not," was his reply, and he told me that life deals us all a set of cards and I just had to deal with it and move on.

I am still trying to live by this suggestion two years on.

The first few weeks were just really getting to know the therapists and nurses, and finding out more about what my goals were and what I wanted to achieve. A full and quick recovery of course!

I immediately set myself a target of six months that I was prepared to stay there and work hard, any longer would have to be negotiated nearer the time (as if I really had a choice in the matter!). We had already booked our first family holiday in September at Oasis in Penrith. We had booked it when I was pregnant and I was looking forward to walking around the lake. As I got slightly better, walking around the lake became a target for me to work towards. My aim was to be back at home to prepare for our first family holiday with Daniel.

A Taste of
Home Life

Again I had started to build relationships with the nurses and I called them all by their individual names. After all this time in hospital, I had cottoned on that if you wanted some assistance it was a good way to ensure they put you before someone else and their requirements! It was also a good memory test for me and got the grey matter working again.

After I had been there a few weeks and had progressed in my recovery somewhat, Dr Downton decided that I could be allowed home for my first full weekend visit. She checked that Dom was happy to be responsible for me over the weekend (as I was still quite poorly and a bit of a liability!) and arranged that he could come in to one of my physiotherapy sessions, so that he would be familiar with the way I transferred from my wheelchair to his car.

At this time I was still heavily reliant on my wheelchair. Since being admitted to Cherry Tree I had been given a new one on loan and was told that I would soon be measured for one that I could keep indefinitely. We therefore decided that we needed to make changes at home to accommodate me over the weekend. Dom had to bring down the spare beds from upstairs and we put them in the playroom, so that I would have access to the downstairs loo in the night should I need it.

It felt really good to be home, but also strange not to be in our own bed upstairs. Anyway it was just nice to be able to canoodle again even though it was not ideal as we were on the spare beds, which were two single ones that could be pushed together, and there was a big gorge in the middle!

I desperately wanted to go upstairs to see Daniel in his bedroom, and tuck Emily in at night and read her a story. Dominic said I would soon build up to it.

On this first proper home visit, I realised that since we had had Daniel, we had quickly outgrown the new house. I still had not been able to make my mark on the house as I had planned, because I had either been pregnant or ill while we were living there. The walls were all still the colour magnolia, which is the standard colour of paint that builders use for brand new houses. Also now that we had two children and all their belongings, any initial extra space had been taken over by little people, their toys and equipment.

I can vividly remember that on our way home Dom needed to get some food shopping for the weekend. We called at the Co-op shop in Hazel Grove. Dom left us all in the car and dashed to get the few items we needed. He was only gone five minutes, but it felt like hours. I felt very vulnerable and because I could not walk far, my mind went into overdrive and I thought of lots of possible scenarios that could happen and leave me in trouble. Daniel started crying for his daddy and I realised that they had become inseparable. Emily was fed up, so I tried to get her to sing some songs or count the passing cars. I then discovered that it can be quite hard to console young children when you don't have the physical ability to lift them up and hug them.

From the car park we could see the busy A6 road and the cars, buses and trucks seemed to be racing and whizzing past. The world seemed a very frightening and noisy place after the tranquil purpose-built hospital I had been in for the last few weeks. I started to wonder how I would ever cope in the real world again if I was ever discharged from hospital.

When we got home things were not much better. I found it hard to cope with the noise of the children playing. The raindrops were pattering on the window outside. Dom had switched on the television, as it was Grand National day. This in itself seemed a problem for me because the screen was showing the race, but also had information about the runners and riders across the bottom of the screen, and I remember thinking that my brain could not deal with the two sets of information. When the telephone started to ring as well, I put my head in my hands and said to Dom that I wanted to go back to the hospital. He was really understanding and said that it would take me a while to adjust, but if that was what I wanted, to come home every single weekend, I would have to really work at it. I just could not understand. I had wanted to come home so much, but did not realise that now my own home was outside my comfort zone.

The same thing happened the next day when we went to my mum's house. It was a traditional thing that Dom and I took our children, and my brother and his wife took their two children, for a light lunch every Sunday. Laura and Michael, my niece and nephew, were particularly well behaved that day, but I could not cope with them not staying still for more than a second, as all children typically do. They were not particularly noisy, but again I found it hard to cope. There was too much going on for my brain to process. Again Dom said it was a barrier that I would have to go through if I wanted to see Laura and Michael, my niece and nephew, every weekend. I did not want to become miserable old Auntie Jane at only age thirty-two, so I decided that although I had had enough today, I would really work at concentrating next time.

The good thing about being home was that I could eat mountains of toast. Toast was not allowed at Cherry Tree for health and safety reasons and because there were not enough staff to make it for all the patients at breakfast. I had thought this was ridiculous at the time. Most of the patients had had rapid weight loss and were trying to gain weight to make them stronger. I had had toast for breakfast at Stepping Hill, which was part of the same NHS Trust, so I found this totally bizarre.

Anyway, when I returned to the hospital on Sunday evening, I was shocked to find that when Dom wheeled me back through the doors and to my bed that I was actually quite relieved and glad to be back in a safe environment. This was the total opposite reaction than we had both expected. In fact, Dom had arranged for some friends to come and visit me in hospital that evening, as he had thought it would cheer me up after all my tears and the anticlimax of coming back!

It was lovely to see our friends, Trevor and Jane.

"You can do this. Girls called Jane are very strong and fighters. Do it for us," Jane said, giving me a much-needed confidence boost.

This was also a source of inspiration to me and I decided that I would have to pretend to myself that I was just away on a course with work. I would go home every weekend and familiarise myself with being there, and I would come back to the safe zone of the hospital during the week for all my therapies for however long it took. This concept sounded fine. The reality was much tougher than I had ever imagined.

As the first weekend had gone relatively well, I was then allowed home every weekend. A few weeks after I had been admitted to Cherry Tree it was Emily's second birthday and we had planned to have a small family party for her on the nearest weekend to the sixteenth of April. We all gathered around to sing 'Happy Birthday' to Emily at her party and I was so overwhelmed that I burst into tears. Emily did not understand why her mummy had started crying when it was her birthday and it was supposed to be a happy time, and I had to assure her that everything was fine. I also felt a little embarrassed as my brother and two brother-in-laws were there and probably did not understand where I was coming from.

As the weekends went by I developed confidence at home and was able to concentrate on things a little better. It started to feel more like the home I had remembered and where I so desperately wanted to be. I even became so confident that I would go upstairs. Dominic would carry me up so I could look at the children in bed and I would come down the stairs on my bum.

Emily thought this was a fantastic game to play. Daddy stood at the bottom of the stairs and Emily and I would take turns in going down a step on our bottoms. At the same time Dom would commentate and say:

"Emily bumpety-bump, now Mummy bumpety-bump."

The Bumpety bump game

~

It was also good going home at weekends because I would also see my friends, Trevor and Caroline, who had bought a new house on the estate just around the corner from us. They always made me feel as though I was doing well, and quite often we would go around for a barbecue or a meal, and they would take the pressure off by helping us with the kids, who both doted on them, especially Caroline! Also Trevor was Daniel's hero as he had a real motorbike in his garage!

~

After I had been in Cherry Tree a week, they decided to move me to a room of my own. I was really chuffed. I would now have some privacy. They moved me to Room 3, which was up at the other end of the hospital near the dining room.

JANE COUPES

The downside of moving there was that things were pretty quiet and it was a bit lonely unless it was near a mealtime and then you could hear people making their way up to the dining room (either slowly on foot or in their wheelchairs).

The upside was that all the single rooms had their own televisions, donated by the local constabulary. When I had been on the ward there had been one television between four of us. I wasn't really well enough to watch TV and concentrate then, but the two older ladies used to have arguments about what channel they would watch!

I soon settled in my new room, although at night you could hear the nurses walking up and down the corridor. I used to joke to my visitors and say that if I was a manager in a hospital trust, I would ban noisy shoes for nurses at night! I would use my new compact disc player and headphones to drown out the noises and the endless buzzers that used to go off in the night. Thank heavens for the band Westlife and Simon & Garfunkel, my relaxing night listening.

After I had been there three weeks, I discovered why they had moved me to a room so quickly. I knew that I had been doing really well in all my therapy sessions, but there had to be more to it. One spring day Dom came to visit and told me that he had good news. He then told me that Juliet, the ward manager, had said that to enable him to return to work full-time, she had arranged that Daniel could come in during the days and that I would look after him as the hugest and most important part of my rehabilitation, with some assistance from the nurses. I was over the moon.

I had really missed out on one-to-one time with Daniel and it used to really hurt me when people would ask about his progress. I was his mum and I didn't even know if he was smiling yet, what his sleeping patterns were or if he was focusing on objects etc. We had not been alone together properly since 24th February when he was born! I could not wait to get my hands on him and give him a big hug.

Dom's Auntie Angela had started visiting me regularly in hospital and she used to always bring home-baked Tiffin, which I loved. She remembers a time when she called and I had Daniel with me. She admired the outfit that he was wearing and I said:

"Yes, that one is nice. I haven't seen it before."

Angela knew from all her years as a midwife that it is usually the mother who chooses a child's clothes to put on in the morning and she felt a little sad that I was missing out on those little decisions. However, in our unique situation Dom had to choose Daniel's clothes and put them in the bag before he dropped him off at the hospital.

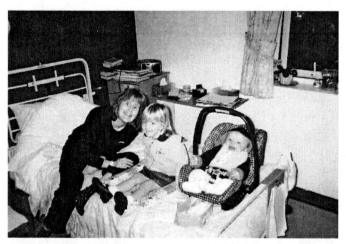

Morning drop off time

~

We began to make arrangements. We borrowed a baby bath and changing mat from my friend, Michelle, with the twins. When I went home that weekend we went to Sainsburys and bought baby supplies - nappies, wipes and nappy sacks - for me to keep in my room. Dom arranged a timetable with our families, so that he would drop Daniel off at eight thirty every morning and someone would pick him up at two thirty each afternoon and keep him until Dom got home about 6 o'clock.

The timetable was like this:-

DAY	PERSON COLLECTING DANIEL
Monday	My mum and dad
Tuesday	Nicki - my sister-in-law
Wednesday	My mum and Auntie Doreen
Thursday	Nicki - my sister-in-law
Friday	Dom's mum and dad

Consequently, all these family members became extremely close to Daniel and were a huge part of his life, and I will always be eternally grateful to them that they cared for my son when I was too ill to do so. However, at the time it was gut-wrenching and extremely difficult for me to hand him over at two thirty each day, and when he had gone I felt an emptiness that I had never ever experienced before.

~

The weekend we went on our baby equipment expedition

was a story in itself. We decided to go to a Sainsburys store at Handforth Dean, which was next to a John Lewis store. We went in the Sainsburys store first. Dom got a wheelchair trolley for us and attached it to my chair. He was pushing me and I steered Daniel haphazardly in his buggy with Emily sitting on my knee. We were practically the length of a freight train from beginning to end. When we turned the corners to go from aisle to aisle it was like something out of a cartoon as we nearly knocked innocent shoppers flying!

Next we went to John Lewis, and after we had finished shopping Dom left me near the foyer while he went to put the shopping away and put the kids in the car. He said he would drive around and pick me up in the lay-by outside. I immediately felt very vulnerable in my wheelchair. What if he doesn't come back for me? I thought, together with lots of other paranoid things like. What if I need the loo while I am waiting for him?

I then topped it off by trying to do a spectacular transfer from my wheelchair back into the car. My physio, Mike, had asked me to put my right arm in the air when standing up, in a 'Saturday Night Fever' style to help me to transfer my weight correctly. This was fine in the gym in hospital, but I got some very strange looks outside John Lewis!

"What if we bump into someone we know whilst we are shopping?" I had said to Dom prior to the trip.

I was a bit bothered about being seen out and about in my wheelchair, but Dom helped me to resolve these doubts.

"Jane, you can't walk very far, so unless you want to stay indoors all the time and never go shopping you will just have to get on with it in your chair."

He was right and this was another situation where I just had to bite my lip and carry on, but I didn't like it.

~

All of a sudden at the hospital there seemed to be an influx of extra staff, and because of this the nurses took it in turns to organise entertainment after the evening meal. We had quiz nights, bingo nights, video nights and also a karaoke evening. These were all a great success and enabled the patients to get to know each other a bit better. I was very competitive and won prizes at the bingo evening and also the quiz night.

On the karaoke night, my cousin, Paul, his wife and their son, David, called to visit me. They came into the television room where it was taking place and I think they were a little bit taken aback, but they joined in anyway! After they had left I joined in singing to the different songs with the nurses. It was all going well. It got to around 8.45 p.m., the end of the shift for most of the nurses, and things went a little bit quiet. They had left the equipment, so we carried on. Eventually there were only two patients left. There was myself and an Asian guy, who I shall call Mohammed. He was a nice guy who had been in Cherry Tree for nearly two years after a road traffic accident. He was learning English and it was improving all the time, as he was so inquisitive.

I decided to take responsibility for ensuring that the evening did not go flat, so I switched on the next song. It was 'Bee Bop a Luh La' and I motioned to Mohammed to sing it. He was really struggling with the alien words, so I joined in and we did a duet. This was very uncharacteristic of me, as I had been painfully shy sometimes, but I was having a giggle and in my now very boring and mundane life this was a breath of fresh air.

We carried on singing and the next song was Stevie Wonder with 'I Just Called to say I Love You'. I was feeling brave, so grabbed the microphone from Mohammed and did a very bad solo effort. Just then Dom came into the room. He had a big grin on his face, for he had already heard me from down the corridor. He knew me really well, and in all the time I had known him I had done karaoke, but always in a group after a few beers. Never a solo when I was stone cold sober!

He later went on to tell me that he had read a leaflet that he had picked up in the reception area of the hospital, and it had said when you have a stroke it can drastically alter aspects of your personality and make you lose any inhibitions! How true this must be!

The extra influx of staff also meant that I could have a nurse who was dedicated to helping me to look after Daniel for the day. Juliet, the ward manager, had asked all the nurses for volunteers to help look after a post-natal mum and her new baby. I later found out that she had been inundated with requests to do what became known as 'baby duty.'

A few of the younger nurses were apprehensive, but keen to have a cuddle with Daniel. All patients in a hospital are totally unique, but I truly was in a different way, as I was the only one with a baby to look after as well as getting better and doing well in all my therapies.

We soon got into a bit of a routine, which is so important with a new baby. I would have a nurse allocated to me, who would assist me on a weekly basis. The timetable was kept to where possible, so I had some continuity. All the nurses were brilliant with both Daniel and me, but I still had my favourites and ones that I looked forward to spending time with more than others.

Dominic would drop Daniel off at 8.30 a.m., so I had to make sure I was showered and had eaten my breakfast by then. We would then give Daniel his breakfast, bath him, dress him, take him for a walk in the hospital grounds and generally amuse him. I had to learn to do all these things predominantly with one hand and that is why there was always a nurse on hand to assist where I physically just couldn't quite complete a task. The nurses would look after Daniel while I went into my therapies and sometimes when I had my meals. Obviously sometimes I had to break off from my meal if he needed a nappy change or a feed! This became the daily routine, and during Daniel's quiet times I would chat with the allocated nurse for that week while my son slept.

At the hospital there was a multisensory room with a double heated waterbed in it. It had several bubble tubes and you could also have different light effects in the room, which were projected onto the walls. Quite often we would take Daniel in there and it was lovely to lie on the bed with him, listen to relaxing music and watch the lights. Sometimes a nurse called Sue used to do aromatherapy on me at the same time. There was no clock in the room, so it was quite easy to lose a whole afternoon in there. Was it really Daniel or me who chose to go in there so often?

Daniel caused a huge stir around the hospital. Everywhere I went people, patients, visitors or staff would coo over him. Lots of the staff went very broody and wanted endless cuddles with him. He loved all the attention and played to the crowd, smiling and gurgling.

Sometimes I would feel quite stressed when I had Daniel with me. This was because I felt that I had to fit his routine around my therapies, i.e. make sure he was asleep when it was physio or occupational therapy. I felt like it was quite hard to fit a baby into the hospital routine. I was constantly thinking that it was an unreal situation. In the real world if Daniel had been playing up, I could have cancelled a coffee with friends or a trip to the shops, but in hospital I felt a huge responsibility to be on time and able to put 100 per cent into my therapies. An overriding emotion was that I kept comparing it with the time Emily and I had when she was small. There were no shopping trips, walks in the park or visits to the clinic for Daniel. I felt we were trapped in a hospital routine that we could not break until I was fitter. I felt it was a vicious circle, as Daniel and Emily were my huge reasons to get better, but sometimes with Daniel in hospital with me all day I felt I was not totally concentrating on my physio or occupational therapy, as I was always aware that Daniel might need his next bottle or a nappy change. Without full input into my sessions I felt I would never get better and, therefore, be set free from hospital! Catch-22 situation or what?

Even though sometimes the nurses would take over if he played up, I still could not concentrate fully as he was my baby and I wanted to be involved in all his care. In hindsight I have realised that I was just subjected to the pressure that every new mum feels, but under very different circumstances. I suppose up until I had arrived at Cherry Tree and Daniel had started to spend the days with me, I had almost been protected from the responsibility I had, i.e. a new son and all that brings with it.

One day I had Daniel on my lap while he was asleep and Dominic was pushing me into the hospital gardens in my wheelchair. Emily was galloping behind. Just as we came to the reception area we turned the corner and there stood a nun. She commented on Daniel saying how lovely he was and asked about what had happened to me. She then told me that she regularly visited the hospital to give Holy Communion to the patients. She asked me if I would like her to visit me and I immediately said yes. Dominic commented on this. Although we are both Catholic, we are not necessarily fully practising ones any more.

"I need everybody on my side at the moment," I said, and he agreed.

Although I did not always go to church on a Sunday at the time, that didn't mean that I didn't pray regularly. Since I had ended up in hospital I had taken to saying a different prayer every night in the darkened ward and it went something like this:-

> Dear Lord
> Thank you for my life.
> Thank you for Emily and Daniel
> Thank you for Dominic and our families.
> Please give me the strength to see this thing through and please make my left arm work soon.
> Amen

After this Sister Margaret would visit me every time she visited the hospital. She would give me Holy Communion and would also read me passages from the *Bible* and give me some hope. She had a lovely, soft lilting Irish accent and I used to feel particularly relaxed when she was praying with me in my room. I could have listened to her voice for hours and hours.

I just had to hope that a combination of my own prayers, Sister Margaret's prayers and the prayers of practically the whole of the Catholic faith in Stockport, would generate some divine intervention and make my taste of home life and motherhood become a reality again soon!

'The Science Bit'

In terms of what happened to me, there are essentially four conditions to deal with. I have, therefore, included some facts about the different conditions in order to explain them.

Primarily I had Crohn's disease, which was diagnosed at the age of seventeen. This affects 60,000 people in the UK. Research shows that the number of people with Crohn's disease has been rising steadily, particularly among young people. More recently numbers have stabilised.

Crohn's disease can affect anywhere from the mouth to the anus, but mostly affects the small intestine and/or colon. It causes inflammation, deep ulcers and scarring to the walls of the intestine. The main symptoms are abdominal pain, weight loss, general tiredness and sometimes urgent diarrhoea. In my case it affects exactly where the small and large intestines join and means when I get severe pain it is always on my right side in exactly the same place. It also affects my body's ability to absorb nutrients from my diet, especially fat and iron in my case. Consequently, I have always been fairly slim, but always low on energy, requiring power naps or rests as necessary!

During my first pregnancy my Crohn's went completely into remission. The assumption was that during my second pregnancy I would be more susceptible to heart disease because of my Crohn's and this led to me having post-partum cardiomyopathy.

Basically there are four different types of cardiomyopathy; dilated, hypertrophic, restrictive and arrythmogenic. I had dilated cardiomyopathy, which is a disease of the heart, causing it to enlarge and pump less efficiently. The muscle in the heart becomes floppy or weak and the heart becomes unable to pump blood around the body as quickly. In turn, this causes fluid to build up in the lungs, which then become congested, resulting a feeling of breathlessness. This is called 'left ventricular failure' and is why the medical staff kept saying:

"It's her LV function."

In my case the septum (the partition that separates the left and right ventricles - see diagram below) became congested and caused the damage.

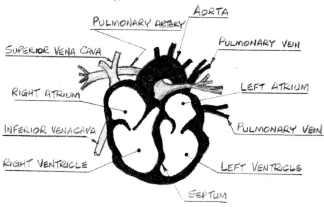

The symptoms of cardiomyopathy are as follows:-

- shortness of breath;
- swelling of ankles;
- palpitations - these are caused by an abnormal heart beat, in my case too quickly, and this is why the medical team kept saying, 'She's tachycardic!' Whilst in hospital I was treated with the drugs, digoxen and silazapril to keep my heart working and to enable it to repair.

The symptoms of Cardio Myopathy can come on slowly, or be very sudden in onset. Every case varies and each individual has different symptoms. I had no previous symptoms and this condition was only made obvious during my second pregnancy, probably because of the extra demands placed on the heart. Because of the heart condition, this in turn led me to have a stroke or CVA (cerebrovascular accident).

It was inferred to me that although the doctors knew I was at risk of having a stroke and took precautions against this, they didn't take into account that when a woman has just delivered a baby, her blood clots quickly, therefore, is stickier to enable her placenta area to heal after the delivery.

A stroke or CVA as the medics call it, refers to a brain injury that occurs when the flow of blood to brain tissue is interrupted, causing brain tissue to die because of lack of nutrients and oxygen.

There are two different types of stroke:

- ischaemic stroke;
- haemorrhagic stroke.

The most common stroke is the ischaemic type caused by a blockage in an artery, which affects blood flow to, or within, the brain. An ischaemic stroke can also be called a TIA (transient ischaemic attack) if it happens for less than 24 hours. These types of stroke account for approximately 90 per cent of strokes, and damage is caused by oxygen starvation to the brain. Haemorrhagic strokes account for the other ten per cent of strokes and these are also known as brain haemorrhages where there is a bleed in the brain. In these types of stroke, the injury occurs where the pressure of the escaping blood and oedema (swelling) damages or destroys brain cells.

There are also events that may be called strokes or CVAs, which have similar results to strokes. The doctors kept talking about a CVA when they spoke about my condition, although my family were just advised that it was a clot to the brain. Brain cells that have died cannot start working again. However, areas of brain affected by swelling may recover as the swelling disappears. The brain is very adaptive and with time can often find new ways to transmit information (new neural pathways) to avoid the damaged areas.

Every single stroke is different, which is what I was told during my time in hospital. As the survivor reacts differently depending on where the brain is affected, what type of stroke and the extent of damage, I guess this is why doctors find it hard to commit to answers about your long-term health.

In my case the stroke resulted in my left arm and leg being totally paralysed to begin with. My speech was affected, but I never lost it completely. The paralysis in my arm and leg meant there was a requirement for me to receive ongoing physiotherapy for several reasons; to get the best recovery possible and also to retain that recovery and prevent my condition from deteriorating. By repeating exercises daily and religiously I was attempting to retrain my brain to develop neural pathways.

The physiotherapists call it a left hemiplegia, which means a weakness on the left side of the body, but it isn't quite as simple as that. Most hemiplegias do not remain a weakness - some muscles become over strong or spastic and some muscles remain weak or flaccid. There can also be probable sensory (feeling, touch, temperature, pressure) disturbances.

Your body is constantly changing or adapting to recovery, which essentially is learning, providing you give the body the opportunity to recover. Hemeplegia does not affect one side of the body; the other side may be affected or just compensating.

Imagine... If you are carrying a heavy bag on one side (see diagram below).

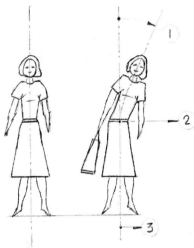

The heavy bag represents the stroke.
1) Pull head away for balance.
2) Flex spine away from bag for balance.
3) Shift weight away from heavy bag to stop it pulling you over.

This is a simplistic view of how the body compensates or adjusts to cope with a hemeplegia (the heavy bag).

When thinking about treatment, the long-term treatment of a person following a hemeplegia is to:

- try to achieve a symmetrical posture;
- remove the 'heavy bag', i.e. lighten the weak side and make it involved with the body's movements;
- minimise the compensations on the 'good' side;
- stimulate balance;
- prevent muscles shortening and tightening;
- prevent joints stiffening;
- look after loose joints;
- improve body awareness and posture.

All exercises or treatment should be orientated around normal functional activities, e.g. walking, dressing, moving from sit to stand.

These changes in your body are very difficult to deal with and can restrict you in every aspect of life; however, people can take one look at you and see you have difficulties and they will sometimes make allowances. What they don't know, or cannot see, is that there are other significant and colossal issues that you have to deal with, and I have identified these as follows.

- Grieving
- Depression
- Fatigue
- Confidence issues

No one can see that you are grieving for the very active person you were before. With every task you face there are hurdles when you have been left with a weakness, and this is very tough to deal with until you eventually discover other ways to get around the tasks that need doing. My consultant actually said to one of my rehab friends:

"You will adapt your life so much, so even if you do get a full recovery, you can never be the same person again!"

As far as depression goes, I feel that I have mostly had a positive outlook and kept focused on getting better; however, there were also days (usually around my menstrual cycle) when I couldn't stay focused and felt really low. This wasn't helped by the third factor that no one can see - the fatigue that comes after a stroke.

If I have experienced depression, in my case it manifested itself in anxiety. I started to have the most awful anxiety attacks and was, therefore, put on medication to help this. I also feel that a huge element in this was that my brain was no longer functioning in the normal way, which caused a chemical imbalance. A normal functioning brain is a giant messaging system that controls everything from your heartbeat to walking, to your emotions. The brain is made up of billions of nerve cells called neurons. These neurons send and receive messages from the rest of your body, using brain chemicals called neurotransmitters. These brain chemicals - in varying amounts - are responsible for our emotional state. Depression happens when these chemical messages are not delivered correctly between brain cells, disrupting communication.

When you try to open the new neural pathways, your brain is actually working in a very different way to the way in which it was designed. Usually your brain would function in the most effective way, but this is not the case after a stroke, therefore, more energy is used up, consequently, people who have suffered stroke experience a level of fatigue that most people cannot even comprehend.

JANE COUPES

When you are young and you pass your driving test, your instructor tells you that the real learning curve happens when you start to go out and drive by yourself. My learning curve after my stroke started properly when I had to begin doing tasks again by myself at home, and started going out and doing normal everyday activities again. However, the anxiety attacks happened every time I faced doing something that was now out of my comfort zone...

The Steepest
Learning Curve

I truly believe there had already been some divine interven-tion to make me survive that desperate night and actually wake up on the morning of 9th March, 2001. I also started to do well in all my therapies and the progress was very rapid. I will tell you about the different therapies individually, so as not to confuse you.

Firstly, there was physiotherapy, when the task of opening neural pathways began. After going back to basics with Mike, the physiotherapist, and making sure my transfers were near perfect, (hence the 'Saturday Night Fever' arm, to make me shift weight symmetrically through my body) we started to do some more dynamic stuff. I started to go on the exercise bike and gradually build up the resistance to build muscle tone in my legs again. The rest of the patients started to call me 'sparrow legs', as they could not believe that even though my legs were painfully thin they were still strong enough to nearly be on the highest resistance out of anyone.

We also started to work on my balance using a wobble board and some exercises to strengthen my trunk (working on my core stability) using a Swiss ball. The experts had said that for someone who had had a stroke and the degree of injuries that I had, my balance was particularly good. I put this down to the fact that I used to do a lot of gymnastics, including high beam work, when I was a little girl. They also confirmed that my body was very crafty, my right side being very clever at overcompensating for my left side and covering it up (this was all going on without any input from me!). We did lots of work on my walking. I had only ever taken a few steps, always with help from a physiotherapist.

After returning one Monday morning after weekend leave, during one of my morning physiotherapy sessions I spoke to Mike.

"I've got a confession to make. I've been taking steps by myself at the weekend."

Mike said that he had known that I would do this at some point.

"Come on, let's go for a walk then," he said, grabbing my hand. "If we hold hands, we'll start a rumour around the hospital and people will talk!"

We did a circuit of the hospital. We then discovered all the bad habits my body had got into and decided which bits we now had to focus and work on. It wasn't as bad as I thought. My left foot now turned in and dragged when I was walking, and we had to work on the length of my strides and make me look normal when walking and not 'like a stiff' as one of the other female physiotherapists had noticed!

I always tried to put 110 per cent effort into my physiotherapy sessions. Sometimes I found it difficult when we were working on my weak arm, or left upper limb as they used to call it. This really annoyed me. 'It's still an arm; it just doesn't work properly right now!' I wanted to scream.

I found it soul-destroying when Mike asked me to move my fingers and I would look at them and will them to move. Sometimes I would be rewarded with a tiny flicker and at other times there was no response whatsoever, despite all my efforts. Hence, the long road to opening neural pathways began and we started to do lots of repetitive movements that I could practise.

I now say that if I had my time again, I would make a good physiotherapist because I know what it was like to be on the receiving end. I know how uncomfortable and hot it is to wear splints on your arm and leg at night and I also know how it totally freaks you out when your body will not do as you instruct it any more.

My left leg started to take on a life of its own and once during a session it began to shake uncontrollably. I looked at Mike then down at my leg.

"I'm not making it move like that!" I said.

He said it was a reaction that can happen when your leg is overtired and it goes into spasm. In addition to this, sometimes if Mike asked me to move my left foot in a certain way, I would try to carry out the required movement, but my right leg would start to move involuntarily and he explained that when you have a weak side, the strong side automatically tries to dominate all movements and will try and take over. It was weird, totally confusing and disorientating.

On a bright sunny day we were doing some work outside in the hospital grounds and I told Mike I was completely shattered. He told me this was a common thing with neurological patients and that they generally suffer from a lot of fatigue, and also I had the added disadvantage that I had the general

JANE COUPES

fatigue that comes after having a new baby, heart problems and having Crohn's disease anyway.

A quadruple whammy for Jane!

Most of the sessions took place in the hospital gym. Another time, Angela, one of the female physiotherapists, was stretching my left arm above my head whilst I lay on a therapy couch.

"Look I am not a wimp! I have delivered two children with very little pain relief, but that really does hurt," I told her.

She explained that my muscles had been inactive for so long that any movement would be excruciatingly painful for a long while. She was just trying to keep the range of movement for my arm, so that it did not cease up completely. I felt as if I was in a torture chamber and she was stretching my arm out of the socket!

As part of my therapy, I was supposed to tap my toes as often as possible, concentrating on my left toes, of course, which were really difficult to tap, wiggle or even move. However, when I went home at the weekends, I used to have the VH1 music channel on as background music, and I remember one day it was on and S Club 7 came on with their song 'Don't Stop Moving.' I was not a huge fan, but this one was really catchy and before I knew it my toes (both feet) were tapping away in time with the beat. When I went back after the weekend, I told Mike that Dr Downton should subscribe the hospital to satellite television, as the music channels were crucial to the patients' recoveries. He reckoned she would not be up for it.

I also found it very strange when we were practising walking in the gym in bare feet. My feet had now become totally reliant on my trainers for support. Strange surfaces, i.e. carpet, concrete etc., now caused problems and made me trip myself up. I could not believe that I had taken these things for granted before my stroke.

Sometimes when I was on weekend leave and we were in public places, I used to just sit on a bench to catch my breath and watch people walking by.

> "Look, they are not even thinking about what they
> are doing," I said to Dom. "Neither did you before
> you were ill," he replied

Now I really had to concentrate on the length of my strides. I had to try and put my heel down before my toe and also try and make sure that my foot did not turn inwards. There was so much to think about that I felt my head would explode!

Another activity that was good therapy for me was to push Linda (one of my rehab friends) around in her wheelchair. Sometimes I would push her down to the therapy rooms, as we quite often had therapies together anyway. It was good practice for me because I was holding on to her wheelchair and this kept my arm, especially my wrist, in a good position. I was also doing lots of walking and concentrating on something else, rather than looking down at my feet to see what they were doing, which I had a tendency to do.

"Does it feel like a normal person is pushing you?" I used to ask Linda.

She would confirm that the speed and pace felt the same as when one of the nurses was pushing her around.

~

Soon after I had been in the hospital I became really fed up with having to ask for assistance every time I needed the loo. I decided that I needed to take some action myself. I had been moved to Room 3 and there was a toilet right across

JANE COUPES

the corridor, so I decided that I was feeling brave one day, so ventured across there by myself.

This was a huge achievement. I could hold on to my bed, my sink and the walls of my room in order to get to my door, then I held on to the door until I was in the corridor. The difficult bit was next. I had to take five whole big steps across the corridor and there was absolutely nothing to hold on to on either side. This was particularly frightening when I found out from one of our group meetings that a high percentage of people who have already had head injuries are most likely to fall and damage themselves again!

Once I was in the toilet I was fine. The toilet had grab rails and bars, having been specifically designed for people with difficulties.

Since being moved to Room 3, I also discovered the benefits of cot sides. My new bed was a lot higher off the floor and my body was now such a dead weight that I was frightened I would fall out. My balance had been affected by my stroke, but also my left arm was so low in tone and heavy that I thought it would pull me out of bed. In actual fact sometimes my arm would flop out of bed with such force that it nearly pulled the rest of me over as well. Attempting to lie on my left side was very frightening too, as I couldn't feel the bed. My brain was totally ignoring my left side, so I kept getting the sensation of falling from a considerable height!

My weight had dramatically dropped and I was told that I needed to put weight on to be stronger and get better. This was something that I could have some control over, so I desperately tried to increase my appetite.

Tuesday morning was the time when all the patients were weighed on the scales. As this was after the weekend, I started to become involved in organising what we had to eat at the weekends at home. I chose lots of things that I really liked and I eventually started to put on a few ounces per week, with the help of lots of Chinese takeaways and roast meals. If I had put weight on I used to do a little cheer. The nurses joked, saying that I must be the only post-natal mum in the entire country to be cheering at putting weight back on. I was now only six stone, so I had a while to go before I got back to nine stone, which had been my fighting weight before Emily and Daniel.

As my strength slowly increased I started to walk a circuit of the hospital grounds every single evening with my dad when he and Mum visited. I would also walk this circuit during the day with Daniel in his pram, accompanied by one of the nurses. The more often I did it the better I became.

~

Throughout the summer I was allowed to go home to my parents' house for tea every Wednesday and then return to the hospital for bedtime. Again Dad walked me home, linking my good arm, and we measured the journey home at just under a mile. This was a phenomenal achievement and, although at that stage we had to take lots of stops (often sitting on a wall or leaning on a lamp post) for me to catch my breath because of my heart condition, we gradually shortened the length of time it took us to walk home.

Although all my physiotherapy sessions were very hard work, I developed a good rapport with the therapists and we did have a laugh alongside working extremely hard. I have an outstanding memory of my physiotherapist, Mike, who used to do an impression of Marilyn Monroe, using a white plastic apron as a prop. He would waft it up into the air and do a little courtesy as the plastic apron gently fell down again.

Once he borrowed some purple false eyelashes too, so it made us giggle during this particular session. Mike called us 'Team Coupes' and I quite liked the sound of that, so adopted it when I spoke about our families.

"I challenge you to an arm wrestle," Mike said on one occasion.

Of course, the catch was that I had to use my weak left arm and he had decided to tap into my competitive side and see if my arm would work under those circumstances. He didn't phase me too much as he was quite a short bloke. Although at first I recall having lots of difficulty, I do believe that with practice I once beat him and took great pleasure in smashing his arm to the table on which we were working!

One time Mike really annoyed me when he tried to give me a kick up the backside and said that I wasn't working hard enough. He then went on to say that when Daniel was asleep each morning, I should be practising my exercises at every waking moment. The nurses were telling me to rest when Daniel rested and with conflicting opinions, and my fatigue so overwhelming, most of the time when Daniel was asleep, I did rest.

I recall the weekend after Mike had said this comment to me and I went home with an 'I'll show him' attitude. I practised my exercises at every possible moment over the weekend. I remember we were playing in the garden with the children and I held on to Emily's slide for balance and practised my repetitive exercises. I spoke to Dom about it and he said that I had to get a balance between the two opinions. Without adequate rest he thought I couldn't channel energy into my recovery, as there would be absolutely no energy at all!

As a mother, your health is pivotal to family life, therefore, I had to try and strike a balance between doing my utmost to aid recovery, whilst also leaving enough energy to care for my family.

Exercises in the garden

"If anyone ever tries to give you one of those little balls that you place in the palm of your hand and then squeeze repeatedly, don't take it from them," Mike said, during one of my very early physiotherapy sessions, whilst working on my left hand,

He went on to explain that whilst they were good in some cases of stroke, in my case it would definitely hinder my progress and attempt to work on the wrong set of muscles. In my case I could very easily clench my left fist into a ball (in fact sometimes my hand seemed to put itself into that position all by itself!). It was opening my hand into a flat palm that I couldn't achieve and had to work on.

As if learning to walk again and realigning all my muscles wasn't enough to deal with, I also learned that my left elbow joint was not working properly and the stroke meant that my upper arm wanted to be in an upright position all the time (almost as if I was holding on to the overhead handles on the trams in Manchester) as my arm was so 'high tone'. Dr Downton decided that it would be beneficial for me to be injected with Botox, known as Botulinum Toxin, type A, which is used to improve muscle tone and reduce pain in the arms, and this would also make it easier for me to get dressed properly. A few of my visitors asked me to try and secrete some Botox for them, so they could later arrange to have it injected into their lips!

Dr Downton stuck the needle into my arm in several places and injected the poisonous liquid. I was then told by the physios that we had to 'optimise' the effects and work hard on my arm for the next month or so before the positive effects of the Botox wore off. Consequently, I channelled my energy into my arm for those four weeks. My walking practice would have to wait.

Unfortunately, it was also around this time that Daniel started to become more aware of his surroundings and develop his character, so now he was always awake during my physiotherapy sessions and he was vying for attention, both from me and the girls on the physio team. Even though I didn't feel that I had optimised the Botox to the full potential because of little interruptions (!), it was beneficial and meant that my arm would now stay in an almost straight relaxed position down by my side. This obviously improved my balance when walking and now meant that I could attempt to swing my arms a little when taking steps, to form a more natural walking pattern.

JANE COUPES

Recovery - The Whole Picture

So, how to solve the problem of a very confused Jane Coupes, who has difficulty with movement, co-ordination and perception, and turn her into that motivated individual that she was before her stroke?

This is where my second therapy type came into play and this was occupational therapy (OT).

I would equate the way a stroke affects your brain to an episode of *Doctor Who* where an alien force takes you as a prisoner and deletes all information from your brain. Therefore, it is the occupational therapist's job to help you to relearn everything!

During these sessions I learned how to do basic skills again like washing and dressing myself. I now discovered techniques to help me to get dressed more easily, using just my right arm. As you can no longer rotate, bend or manoeuvre your weak arm in tricky ways, you have to learn that you always put your weak arm or leg into a garment first and then your strong arm or leg can do all the hard work. After time I became quite adept at this, although I would often do my buttons up wrong on my pyjamas.

Dom used to laugh at me and I really took it to heart.

"Look, I'm a fool; I can't even put my pyjamas on properly," I said.

He would hug me and tell me not to be so hard on myself. It was a bit of a theme though; because I was now putting garments on differently I would quite easily put a T-shirt on back to front, or my knickers on inside out! It became impossible for me to wear an ordinary bra, so instead I had to start wearing those sports vest ones with no fasteners. I couldn't even move my arm never mind bend it behind my back and then use manual dexterity to cope with a bra fastener!

Dom came to drop Daniel off one morning.

"Why have you got a kangaroo on your back?" he asked.

I was wearing my blue and red Kangol top, and the kangaroo sign was supposed to be on the front. I felt so silly, but just adjusted it to the correct way and made a note to check in future.

~

One of my initial OT sessions was actually first thing in the morning straight after breakfast and it involved taking a bath in front of the therapist. This was purely for her to assess any washing/dressing needs I had now that I was weak and had the use of only one arm. It was a good job that I had no issues about my body and was quite confident about stripping off in front of the nurses and therapists, as I had someone watching over me every single time I bathed or showered (in case I collapsed) for the whole duration of my stay in hospital.

It became apparent very early on that I was going to encounter problems washing my hair and keeping it tidy. It was quite long then and was difficult to wash properly using only one arm, plus it was still only weeks since Daniel's birth. Large clumps of my hair started to come out every time I brushed conditioner into my hair in the shower!

I started to learn how to do everyday tasks again like eating and cooking. I also did some work in the kitchen. To start with this was just brewing up and making a light lunch (always cheese on toast for me!). I had just about remembered how to do these things in sequence, but discovered opening jars and packaging was now very difficult. The world of packaging is an unnecessarily cruel one for weak and elderly people. The therapist gave me some equipment to make things slightly easier. I also discovered that when using a fork in my right hand, there was a problem with the last bit of food, as when I pushed it around the plate it would often go over the edge! I couldn't hold any implements in my left hand, as I had totally lost any ability to grip.

My designated occupational therapist had a heart of gold, but sometimes came across in a very abrupt way. We used to call her the Welsh dragon. The therapist used different techniques to help my learning curve, and I have included some examples of tasks below.

One time she asked me to follow a recipe and make some shortbread. I was able to measure exactly four ounces of margarine from memory without using the scales, except to double-check; however, I tipped flour all over the place. I couldn't even tie up the apron that she had given me to protect my clothes. It was one of those plastic hospital aprons, which nurses use for health and safety. Different colours denote different tasks, e.g. food preparation, washing the patients etc.

At this time I had to adapt my philosophy. I had always done every task to the best of my ability ensuring that tasks were completed to beyond perfection! Now I started to be really grateful if I could indeed fully complete a task at all!

Subsequently, we began to do some work on my memory and concentration, so one day she asked me to complete a jigsaw of the British Isles. I started to do it by sorting the pieces into different colours. As I started to position them where they belonged, I discovered that I was actually finding it really difficult to do. I was frustrated, and told one of the nurses afterwards that I didn't see how this was making me better. I would rather have been learning how to iron again or load a washing machine and practising bending down (without falling over!). I wanted to do things that would be useful to me when I eventually got home and I also wanted a fast track out of this place. I didn't think doing jigsaws was useful in real life. Emily and Daniel's jigsaws were all aimed at five year olds and I knew I would have no problems helping them with those. The truth is that she had been testing my concentration and I was cross to find out that it was not brilliant any more!

My therapist then started to get me to do tasks whilst standing at a high desk at the same time. This was known as 'work in standing.'

"Of course I can stand up and complete that task," I said, and then realised that my heart condition was actually getting the better of me and I was actually finding it really tough and very tiring to stand and complete a short task. But I'm still only 32 - it's impossible that I'm struggling to have the stamina to do this, were my exact thoughts.

The rest of the time I found being tested was not a problem. I was keen to prove myself and thought that it actually could be quite fun if I wasn't in hospital and trapped there. As I

JANE COUPES

developed my concentration we started to do word games like Scrabble and Monopoly, for the adding and subtracting aspect of it. I used to joke with my other rehab friends that the job of occupational therapist was an absolute cinch. Anyone could sit and play games with patients. Of course, I have since realised that there was a whole lot more to it behind the scenes!

After a while I started to do some computer work and I found it quite astonishing that even though I had used a computer every day of my working life, I had now forgotten quite a lot of the knowledge that I had built up. I also couldn't see the screen too well; all the icons looked a lot smaller and they seemed to be in the wrong part of the screen to where I remembered. I had endless games of patience to try and improve my concentration, and again this tapped into my competitive side and I would not stop until I had won several times!

As my concentration gradually improved, my therapist would set me tasks. She had discovered that before my stroke I had really liked shopping and also travel, so she would set me little tasks to do relating to these.

Soon the occupational therapists discovered that I had struck up a good relationship with a few of the patients who were mentally quite well, so they used to book our sessions so that we were all in the therapy room together. We had a lot of fun doing craft activities and trying to use our weak arms. As we were not always successful, we tried to keep our spirits up and I think we were a little bit rowdy, but we certainly kept things interesting!

Practising physical and mental skills through crafts and board games was commonplace, and we started with simple activities then moved on to more complicated ones as I progressed.

Non-craft activities were also used as a form of therapy. One example of these was that my therapist pretended to give me some of Dr Downton's money and said I had to buy something from a catalogue for every member of my family and keep within a certain budget. Another task was to cost a holiday for Dominic and myself. I managed to do this, but found it quite difficult to work through the holiday brochures and to remember to add on airport taxes etc. I just had to hope and pray that a holiday for just Dom and me would really materialise at some point in the near future! At this time, I asked Dom's mum if she thought it would ever come off, and she promised to look after the children for us if it did!

Another time, Linda, Julie (my rehab friends) and I were all in the therapy room at the same time. On this occasion we were all doing exercises of the same kind, i.e. costing holidays. Our therapist had put out a selection of brochures and we had to make our choice of destination and cost it. When the therapist went out of the room, Linda spoke to Julie and me.

"Is she taking the Michael here or what?" she asked, pointing to one of the brochures for walking holidays in the Alps!

As all of us were just learning to walk again this seemed like rubbing salt in the wound. We were hysterical and it took us ages before we could speak without giggling.

Once, Linda and I were booked in on corresponding sessions. This time our objective was to play a game of skittles using our bad arms to throw the balls. I went first and I manoeuvred my left arm as if to throw a ball, but when it was extended, my left hand would not release the ball. Linda told me afterwards that at the time she was thinking, Ah, bless,

Jane that looks really easy, I bet I can do better, then it was her turn. Exactly the same thing happened, but of course, with her right arm. The game went on like this for a while and then we progressed to being able to release the balls. This was good. However, we still did not have enough control with our dodgy arms to aim the ball at the skittles. Instead, we hit everything but; the occupational therapy equipment, tables, chairs and even other patients. It was still good therapy because again we were in hysterics.

Orthotics is also another string to an occupational therapist's bow and this involves making splints to correctly align limbs, and thus we made me a splint for my arm. They called it a resting splint, which meant I was supposed to wear it at night-time in bed. As soon as I had come to Cherry Tree I had become aware that I did not know which position to put my arm in at night. I couldn't get comfortable at all. I soon noticed that my hand would bend over, and one of the nurses noted my concern and mentioned about having a splint made. This was to stop my arm and hand being in a permanent hook position. I just could not get my own hand in a good position. It was like an accessory to my body.

The occupational therapist made me a plastic splint that would force my arm to lie in a flat position with my thumb sticking out, therefore, promoting good patterns for my movements. When she made it in a therapy session, she had to heat the plastic up to mould it to my arm. To do this, she had some water in a wok-type pan and I joked with her, asking if we were having a stir-fry!

One of the other occupational therapists was called Amanda and she used to double up as a physio assistant too. I got on really well with her and she loved Emily and Daniel heaps. One day she told me that she thought the Coupes

Team were like a catalogue family. I was flattered, but as my self-esteem was so low I could see why she would say that about Dom, Emily and Daniel - they were all stunning to look at, but I could not see why she would include me in this description.

The third kind of therapy was psychotherapy and I guess was looking after my mental well-being after the stroke. I was given another psychometric test, which basically consisted of testing to see if I still knew my name, address, the date etc. I was then shown a series of cards with diagrams on them and asked to remember if I had already seen one the same during this session. I passed with flying colours. My cognitive thinking had not been affected too much by my stroke. However, we soon discovered that my memory had been affected a little bit. I could remember events from a long time ago, but if asked, I could not tell you what I had eaten for my lunch.

We also had group sessions on a Thursday. This was generally a series of talks, which included detailed information on the brain and how it could be affected by bumps/clots etc., and was given over a couple of weeks. Sometimes we would just have a group chat about how we were all recovering, how we felt about being in hospital etc.

During one of these Thursday afternoon sessions, one of the other patients, whom I shall call Bob, entertained the rest of us by pretending to be a visiting specialist whose expertise was 'the brain.' He had in fact been a GP in real life before he had been taken ill. He put on some goofy glasses and started to tell us about his latest theory. He told us that he had been working on the difference between men and women's brains and why one was focused totally on football and the other, shopping! We were all in hysterics and, even more importantly, we had all stayed awake for this session!

JANE COUPES

In reality I did learn lots of interesting and useful facts during these sessions and I have included some of them below.

We were all just so tired that it was difficult to concentrate on the information. However, from the sessions we learned that this is because when you have a head injury your brain uses something like one fifth of its total power just trying to repair itself. Consequently, all the other things like breathing, talking etc., make it really fatigued.

For the six months duration, this regime was my way of life and I was completely oblivious to the support system happening around me…

~

In the real world outside, Team Coupes had sprung into action. When they were not visiting me on a rotation system, so that I always had lots of visitors calling at different times of the day to ease the boredom, they were trying to make Dominic's life easier by cooking, washing, cleaning and tending to the garden, all so he could go to work, keep some sense of normality and also keep our family afloat.

My mum and dad were not working, so they were always up at the house, Mum shopping and cooking meals and my dad looking after our garden. Then it was time to visit and they came every single day for seven months, after which my dad went straight to our house to babysit Emily and Daniel, so that Dominic could come and visit me in hospital. Dominic's mum and dad, both still working long days, were doing exactly the same duties in any spare time they had. What a great support system to have around you!

Sometimes the fatigue was so bad that I wondered how I would ever get through the day and carry out all my commitments. When Dom came to visit every night around 7 p.m. he would help me put my pyjamas on, and as soon as he left I would get into bed and go to sleep. That didn't necessarily mean that I slept right through the night. I often awoke to go to the loo in the night (I guess you have a weak bladder just after having a baby) then the sounds in the hospital were so different to me that I didn't always go back off to sleep straightaway. I later learned that this was because after a stroke your brain has to learn how to do tasks again from scratch, so my brain was learning how to fall asleep again - just like a new baby has to learn this skill.

I would quite often wake early in the morning, around four or five o'clock. I later learned that this is also quite common in patients who have had heart problems. It was like a medieval form of torture. I felt so tired, but could never get a sound night's sleep. My friends all thought this was a joke, as in the past I was always the one who never had any problem sleeping on a coach or when travelling. I used to fall asleep as soon as my head hit the pillow at night and because of my Crohn's disease and the fatigue that that in itself can cause, I had often taken ten-minute power naps at weekends and on holidays. It was as if my brain just did not know how to switch off any more, and it was so frustrating.

When you have a stroke or head injury, your body has suffered trauma. As a result, it naturally becomes on red alert. This fact was borne out when I was in my room. My hearing became very acute and, although the buzzers were very loud, I could still tell if someone was at the front door of the hospital above the sound. I could even recognise different nurses in the corridor just by their footsteps. Because of this I found it difficult to concentrate when I had visitors. Loud noises or sudden movements around me started to make me feel very jumpy.

Another time, I tried to take a multi-vitamin in tablet form at breakfast. I felt it had not gone down properly. When I could still feel it in my throat during the afternoon, I buzzed and asked one of the nurses about it.

"If you were going to choke, it would have happened by now," she said.

My condition had made me neurotic and paranoid.

～

It was around about this time that I started to have the most awful anxiety attacks. In one of my previous jobs as human resources team leader, I had come across people who had been off work on long-term leave with anxiety/stress; however, I had never encountered anything like it myself. I had experienced difficult situations in my life before as follows.

1. Dominic had asked me to marry him on one Saturday, several years before, and then changed his mind on the Sunday, saying he had a problem with the commitment thing.
2. I had been overlooked for promotion at work when I had physically been covering that specific job on a relief basis already.
3. A relationship had broken down with my ex-boyfriend after five and a half years.

At the time these had seemed like big traumas in my life. After the stroke and the anxiety attacks, they paled into complete insignificance. So what! They have become dim and distant blips that were character building and made me the person I am today.

The anxiety affected me in that I would experience panic attacks and feel like I just wanted to stand up and bolt out of the hospital. Of course this was impossible, as I could only just walk again! I felt as though I was having palpitations and I became concerned, as palpitations were the reason that I had developed a heart condition and ended up in hospital in the first place. The doctors started to listen to my heart again on a regular basis. They assured me that the anxiety was just another part of my recovery and it was me trying to come to terms with the drastic and extreme things that had happened to my body. David Hinds, author of my *After Stroke* book, had obviously experienced it, and he was right in his thoughts that stroke is difficult to deal with and to come to terms with. He had already dealt with it. I hadn't yet!

I asked Derek, the psychotherapist, about the attacks and he gave me some sheets of information about anxiety, which explained why my body was reacting in the way it was. They call it 'the fight or flight syndrome'. This information helped me a little bit and I started to ignore the symptoms. I would start to control them by saying to myself, I am okay. Nothing is going to happen to me. I will just sit here and try to relax and listen to this CD the whole way through.

Sometimes the attacks would happen when I was in my therapy sessions. All the therapists were very sympathetic; they had obviously experienced it many times before. Mike, the physio, tried to teach me some breathing exercises, and the occupational therapist would make me a cup of tea and give me a sugary biscuit until I had calmed down somewhat and was ready to continue with the day's activity.

JANE COUPES

One time my anxiety escalated and I felt very jumpy. Dom was away on a course with work, so I could not contact him easily. I distinctly remember that Dom's mum and dad had Daniel overnight and his mum brought him into hospital, so that we could both take him for his first set of immunisations early that morning. She arrived just after breakfast and I broke down in tears. She gave me a big hug and said that things were bound to be bad while Dom was away.

That afternoon things just got too much for me. I broke down and shut myself in the multisensory room. I was shaking because I was so anxious. I just wanted to go home and get back to my normal life. Around four thirty-ish, there was a knock on the door. I opened it and Dom was there. He was back from his course, which had finished very early. I was really relieved and things immediately started to feel better. Just then Brenda, my favourite nurse, also came into the room. This was perfect timing, as I needed a good friend at that precise moment and felt that she fitted the bill. She took Daniel from me and left me and Dom to talk.

That evening my friend, Jill, came to visit me for the first time since my stroke. I had worked with her a long time before, but we had always stayed in limited contact and exchanged gifts at birthdays and Christmas times, and also the children's birthdays. She has a son called Gareth. I remembered him when he was a toddler and she used to bring him in to work to visit when she was on holiday. Now Gareth is a young adult and he is good with Emily and Daniel. Jill was worried about me, but she told me that I was doing well. I told her that she had called on my worst day yet and I tried to assure her that I hadn't really turned into a shrivelling wreck!

My dad was also visiting that evening. He helped to calm

me down and said that this was my lowest/worst period, probably coupled with the realisation of how my life had changed.

Before I had started to control my anxiety, I had a weekend home visit. I was totally perplexed to find that I still felt very anxious at home. I had attributed the anxiety down to the fact that I didn't want to be in hospital, but had to be, so I could not understand why it was happening at home. This was especially the case, as the weekend before on my home visit I had really started to feel that I was getting better in coping at home.

"It's not *where* you are, it's *how* you are," Dom said.

My friend, Debi, also helped me through this difficult and perplexing time. When she came to visit one Wednesday evening with the other girls, I told them all how I felt.

"You're not in control of this situation," she said. "You've got to stay in hospital even though you don't want to."

She was right. I had needed someone close to me to hit me with the hard truth. At the same time I really didn't like not being in control of my situation and I guess this was around the time that I realised I had been such a control freak before my stroke!

~

After I had been in Cherry Tree about eight weeks, Dr Downton's SHO (senior house officer) changed. The young doctors seemed to work on a rotation system whereby they would have a placement for eight weeks and then move on. All the nurses explained that a new doctor was starting that day, and there was an excited atmosphere and air of anticipation around the hospital. When he came around to meet all the patients I discovered it was the young doctor with twinkling eyes, who had been in the delivery suite when I had first been admitted to hospital days before my stroke in March. He said I looked a whole lot better and said that he had recently seen some of the staff from Stepping Hill and that they had all been wondering how I was getting on at Cherry Tree. I discovered his name was Gareth and that he would be working with Dr Downton for the next eight weeks or so. Things were looking up; with a bit of eye candy around, the weeks would surely fly by now!

I told Gareth about the anxiety attacks, and he was brilliant. He said that he and Dr Downton had decided to put me on a mild antidepressant for a short time.

As the anxiety had stopped me from sleeping at night, he also said that they had decided to prescribe me a mild sedative called Tamazipan.

That day I started to take both the drugs, and that night I could not sleep at all. I tried everything; listening to my music, watching telly, counting backwards from one hundred. I rang Dom at home from my mobile. In the end I went down to the nurses' station and sat with the night nurses all night long. I was very irrational and kept saying things like, 'I am worried about Dom and how he will cope with Emily and Daniel, I am worried that he will lose his job because he is so tired, I am worried about taking the drugs that I have started, I am worried that I have not done the right thing in consenting to take them. I just want to go home to my family.' The night nurses listened and were full of empathy.

I sat with them all night until the morning staff came on at 7 a.m. The hospital was an even scarier place to be awake in at night. There were screams of pain from some patients, screams of anger from others, patients wandering about like zombies, dosed up on sedation drugs, going to the loo, endless buzzers. It was awful and very frightening.

The next day I felt terrible and was very fatigued. I still had commitments, in that I had therapies to attend and Daniel to look after. The nurses helped me out a bit more that day, as they said that under normal circumstances, if I had had such a bad night, I would have probably asked my mum to come around and help me care for Daniel. They were right.

The physio decided I was going to tackle the stairs in the main building of the hospital. I told Sam that I felt as if I was there in body, but not in mind, so she went easy on me. However, I still managed to walk up a complete flight of stairs, not just a couple of mock steps that I had been doing in the gym. If I could achieve that with no sleep, what could I do when I had experienced a sound night's sleep!

Soon after, the new doctor, Graham, came to do my post-natal check and he said that he would arrange a smear test with my own GP. His next question was enquiring about what we were doing about contraception, which is a standard question they ask at this time. I joked and said that I had the best possible form of contraception because my husband was at home and I was in hospital!

In truth, as I was now having regular weekend home visits, I told Graham that this was becoming an issue and one that Dom and I would discuss and let him and Dr Downton know our decision. I had already been advised that it would not be wise to have another pregnancy, as it could be fatal for me. Dr Downton and Graham suggested that I had a coil fitted. Dr Lewis had already said that he would not allow me to go on the pill or be sterilised because of health risks and implications, so he suggested Dom have a vasectomy. After this meeting with Dr Lewis I sent Dom a text message with the outcome and he replied straightaway. 'You can tell Dr Lewis where to go!' He had a work colleague who had experienced a bad time after a vasectomy and this is what provoked this response!

~

During one of our group therapy sessions a few weeks into the course, one of the older patients in the hospital broke down and told us that she felt very humbled by her experience of being rushed into hospital at short notice. She said her husband was always visiting her, telling her that numerous friends and family had been asking after her health. I fully related to this, as I was in the same situation.

I have said before that I had asked Dom if I was such a horrible person that I deserved all this. The stir I caused within our friends and family was overwhelming. Dominic was forever bringing me letters, cards and best wishes from people who were enquiring after my well-being. My mum and dad constantly told me of people who were praying for me, friends who had brought holy water from Lourdes etc. It seemed that every single faith in the Manchester area was praying for me. I therefore convinced myself that I must have had some good qualities before my stroke.

When your body has suffered trauma, your automatic responses are the first to come back. This is why when people have been in comas for a long time, quite often the first words they will say are swear words! I soon became aware that some of my automatic responses were coming back, including me sometimes swearing! I have an aversion and revulsion about swearing, but really sometimes struggled to control what sounds came out of my mouth in a Tourettestype way! Maybe it was the surroundings of the hospital or the sheer frustration that I had lost all my life choices.

Other automatic responses also started to occur. One day during the summer Emily and Dom had come into hospital for Dom to attend one of my physio sessions. Anyway, Emily ran away from me towards the room where the ward cats were kept. The cats were called Samson and Delilah; they were a new thing and were good therapy for most of the patients. I didn't like cats that much, but Emily and Daniel adored them. Emily would always ask to go and see them, but as soon as the cats ventured out of the meeting room where they were kept, she would run for it.

This exact occurrence had happened on this day and as Emily ran away from the cats, I felt myself chasing after her. I say chasing, but I could not run. However, my walking was as quick as it had ever been since my stroke and it felt for the first time as though it was natural. Mike said it was one of these automatic responses and, as I needed to protect my child to make sure she didn't come to harm in the hospital, my body had responded in the appropriate way, despite my difficulties. Dominic was watching down the other end of the corridor and he said that my steps and strides were near perfect!

Emily obviously brought out my automatic responses because later on when I went home one weekend, I was reading stories and singing to her in bed early one morning. We had read lots of stories and then we moved on to singing. We sang the song that goes 'one, two, three, four, five, once I caught a fish alive.' I was teaching her to count, so did the actions on my right hand. When it came to the next line, 'six, seven, eight, nine, ten,' I was astonished that all the fingers on my left hand did a tiny flicker. The movement was very small, but it was in fact, movement! I was so excited I shouted Dom to come upstairs and see. I practised it all that day, as I was worried that if I stopped, they would never move again. This was the first time that my fingers had moved independently since my stroke and it was a very reassuring, hopeful and forward-thinking moment.

When I got back to hospital the following week, I showed Mike in my physio session and he was really pleased for me.

~

I also had speech therapy (where we worked on sentence structure and also me being able to put inflection into my voice and sentences again). I also tried to make my voice louder, but as I've always been fairly quietly spoken, this was quite a feat. We also did more work on trying to get my smile back, so I completed more exercises to strengthen my cheek muscles. The best therapy was aromatherapy to help my muscles to learn to relax and also the rest of my body (now it was on red alert after the trauma it had suffered)!

My locker photo

These therapies all ran concurrently and we worked on all aspects every single day, except Wednesday mornings, when the staff from the individual disciplines got together and held a meeting with Dr Downton to discuss every patient and their progress. This meant that she was fully aware of every single patient's progress and could chat at length when she did her hospital rounds every Thursday morning.

The support I had around me was all well and good, but inevitably there came a point where no matter how much support I had I realised that, although they all visited frequently, they obviously could not be there during my therapies. I realised I had to find something from inside me that would enable me to continue with my quest for a total recovery. Although family and friends were around they were

JANE COUPES

not able to make my left arm and leg move for me, so it was down to me. I taped a photograph of Dom, Emily, Daniel and myself on my locker next to my bed to help me through the bad times and to spur me on.

I Predict a Riot!

At this point, I have decided to give you a small character analysis of the other inmates (sorry patients!) who I was in effect living with for six months. This is just to give an indication of what things were like for me. I have changed all their names to protect their real identities!

I also want to reiterate that I didn't know any of the patients beforehand, so I can only assume that the severity of their head injuries made them behave in the way they did! Head injuries affect people in awful ways, and I hope I have demonstrated this in the rest of this chapter.

Mohammed's English was progressing really quickly and the nurses constantly tried to make him aware of new vocabulary and British traditions etc. It made me laugh around Easter time when the nurses brought in some hot cross buns for the patients to have at breakfast. He asked what they were and the nurse in question told him that it was bread with fruit in it. He looked very puzzled and when she then tried to tell him about the Easter bunny leaving chocolate eggs in the garden for children, he looked at her as if she had gone off her rocker! Mohammed had also been a patient for the longest time in the Devonshire (nearly two years!). Because of this he had a notion that he was in charge of the hospital, and used to sit at the nurses' station monitoring the buzzer system, delegating and telling the nurses which patients needed assistance.

On our bingo night I was sitting at a table near Mohammed and one of the nurses had explained the purpose of the game to him. He was doing really well and marking numbers off his card then all of a sudden he shouted at the top of his voice, 'my home'. The nurse who was organising the game said, 'what is it, Mohammed?' and he said, 'I have won'. I was giggling quietly to myself, as I realised what he had done. The nurse said to him, when you have marked off all the numbers, you shout 'house'.

"Now I see," he said, but still insisted on shouting 'my home' every single time he won a game.

Another patient who had a serious head injury was quite entertaining. I shall call her Maggie. She was very unstable and she was one of the patients who was guilty of throwing items, swearing and trashing her room from time to time. One day things got pretty bad and she wrecked her room, pulling down the curtains together with curtain rail, and stormed off with her bedding into the foyer of the hospital. She set up camp behind the pool table with her bed covers on the floor. She was, however, still visible when visitors were coming in and out of the building and I don't think she created a brilliant impression!

That night I was sitting reading my book in bed, (*Bridget Jones's Diary*, I think), whilst waiting for the nurses to come around with the drugs trolley with my evening medication. I was quite engrossed (as much as my concentration levels would allow!) in the book, but even that could not hold my attention above the drama in the hospital. Maggie was shouting down the corridor at the top of her voice that she wanted to go home and she would ring a taxi and discharge herself. The nurses got involved in a long conversation explaining that she could not do this without signing a consent form to discharge herself, and without seeing Dr Downton. As it was 9 p.m. Dr Downton was not on the hospital premises, so the debate continued.

I heard Maggie trying to fight her case.

"Maggie, I cannot allow you to go back to an empty house," said one of the nurses.

Maggie replied straightaway.

"The house won't be empty because I'll be in it!"

I could not contain myself from giggling. I thought that as mad as her condition had made her, she was actually quite right in her thought process.

Another time, she was attempting a crossword with one of the male psychiatric nurses.

"Right then, Maggie, this word is five letters long and begins with the letter 's.' The clue is that it is an item of clothing," he said.

She came back to him straightaway.

"It's *shroud*."

"That isn't an item of clothing," the male nurse said.

"It is if you are dead," Maggie responded.

Again she was right. She might have been as mad as a hatter, but she was damned quick! In addition to having a quick mind, she was also very nifty on her feet. Her illness seemed to have only affected her mental stability. Because of this and as she was so unhappy, she escaped from the hospital twice. One time she got stuck in the bedroom window frame and the fire brigade were called out to rescue her. The next time she was more successful, and the police eventually found her a few miles away from the hospital. These attempts both happened some time in May, just after Maggie found out that her house had been repossessed!

One of the elderly ladies on the ward had been hoisted out of her bed so that she could have some physiotherapy. Later that evening when my dad came to visit me, she told him that she had been on a helicopter ride and could he give her a lift home now!

Another victim of a road traffic accident was a young black guy called Wes. He had also sustained bad head injuries and he used a motorised wheelchair. He was very good-looking, had a lovely smile and always seemed really positive to me.

My friend, Michelle, came on another visit, and while she was there I was telling her all about Wes.

"He is a young black guy, wears an eye patch and he drives a motorised wheelchair," I told her.

"I know who he is," Michelle said. "He has just nearly run me over in the corridor!"

He was a bit of a liability in his chair. One of the other patients named him 'demolition man', as he did wreak havoc with the motorised wheelchair. The nickname stuck like glue. You could see damaged skirting boards and doors around the hospital, and he was the guilty party.

I could fully appreciate how difficult these chairs were to operate, as the physio, Mike, had tried to give me one to make me more independent, before I had ventured across to the loo all by myself. It was really difficult to drive and manoeuvre around corners, through doors etc., (no this was not just because I was a woman driver, contrary to popular belief) so I ditched the idea straightaway.

There was another guy, whom I shall call Terry. He shared a room with Wes. He had long dark hair and he always had it tied back. He reminded me of a Sioux Red Indian. When I used to walk Daniel around the building in his pram, Terry always used to comment on what a fantastic life Daniel had, sleeping and eating most of the time.

Adrian was a young lad who again had had a serious head injury after a fall. He had ended up in a wheelchair and his eyes had been badly damaged. When I arrived in the hospital, he was quiet, but as time went on he started to go through the 'truculent schoolboy' phase of his recovery. He would do outrageous things to attract attention. He would follow the drugs trolley around at night demanding his medication. He threw food around in the dining room, trashed the hospital, pulled signs down and threw all the stationery in the foyer all over the show. I felt sorry for him, but he was a real pain and because the nurses had to be on extra alert to make sure Adrian and Maggie did not escape over the perimeter fence, the rest of the patients received less care/time as the nurses were pushed to the limit!

Once when he was in the middle of a rant at night, he fell into my door. I thought he was trying to get in and I was terrified. The nurses were struggling to contain him. A few minutes later I bravely stepped into the corridor and shouted at the top of my weak voice.

"Adrian, stop being noisy, I've got my baby asleep in there."

I pointed into my room. He then started to calm down somewhat. The nurses thanked me for my quick thinking. Of course, Daniel wasn't really there, he was safely at home with Dom, but Adrian didn't know that.

Yet another patient was a young Irish girl, whom I shall call Sinead. She had also been involved in a car accident in the Republic of Ireland and she had serious mental problems. She was lovely, and I started to sit next to her at mealtimes. She was in the room next to mine, so we became friends of a fashion. She loved the children and would let me take them into her room to see her goldfish. However, she could not remember their names no matter how many times I told her.

At mealtimes it was a bit like the film, *Groundhog Day*, in which a man lives the same day and sequence of events over and over again.

'What happened to you?' she would ask at every single meal.

I would explain to her in detail.

'I'm so sorry,' she would say.

This became a bit wearing after the first few times, but I could forgive her, as she was such a lovely girl.

When Linda arrived a few weeks after me, she also got talking to Sinead.

"You can tell me all your secrets," Sinead told Linda, then she paused for a few seconds, "because I won't remember any of them!"

Sinead was also a musician in an Irish band and she would play their music over and over again all day.

Then there was Simon. We used to call him an impostor. He had been involved in a car accident and, although he had serious memory and psychological problems, he looked quite healthy. You could always tell when he was walking down the corridor, as he was the only one who walked at a normal speed and had the sound of normal footsteps. Physically he was fitter than any of us and his gym sessions were even more intensive.

As I became fitter I was allowed to go into the gym by myself to do my exercises and use the exercise bike. Quite often

Simon would be in there at a similar time. I had noticed that every time he was in his occupational therapy sessions, he was always gardening - either clearing up the hospital gardens or tending his own herb garden in a small corner near the therapy rooms. During one of the afternoon gym sessions I joked with him and the other physiotherapists, who were in the gym doing paperwork. I said that he was really an impostor in the hospital and that instead of doing gardening as a therapy, he was secretly growing marijuana. Of course this was all complete nonsense.

Then there were four of us who felt quite sane compared with the other patients. Our illnesses had affected us in a mostly physical way.

~

In May, after I had been at Cherry Tree for about six weeks, Brenda, by now my favourite nurse, told me that another young lady was being transferred to the hospital. She had also had a stroke and had two young children. When this new lady, Linda, arrived at Cherry Tree I asked Brenda to introduce me to her. She had been put into Room 7, which was just along the corridor from me. I asked to be escorted to her room one afternoon and I introduced myself. I remember we chatted for ages and told each other our individual stories. We immediately got on. Linda was just really normal like me. She had had her stroke a while after me. I immediately felt that because we had something so drastic in common, we had a huge bond.

Her stroke had affected her right side and we joked that if we stuck together we would have two good arms and legs. We became a bit of an inspiration to each other. She saw me as being six weeks ahead of her and nearly walking again, and I could look at her in her wheelchair and realise how far I had come.

When we were chatting, we decided that we must have met before in our previous lives because we had both been members at the same gym in Hyde and we were also both members at the same local nightclub in Bredbury!

As beds in this rehab centre were so sought after, we soon got an influx of new patients. I particularly remember that one Wednesday at lunchtime, two new ladies were chatting to each other. They were catching up, as they had both been transferred from the same hospital in Salford and had been on the same ward there. The younger one was crying, as she was so relieved to be at Cherry Tree now, so she could get on with her recovery. They soon became good friends of Linda and me, and we learned that they were called Julie and Suzannah.

The four of us would all get together when we had no therapies to attend. We tried to coincide these get-togethers with the times that the tea trolley came around, so we could have a brew and a chat. Julie discovered a game in her occupational therapy sessions called 'Triominos'. It was like dominoes, but in keeping with the name of the game, the pieces had three sides and three sets of numbers. We started to have games of it in the dining room when it was not in use and we decided that we were being sociable as well as working on our concentration skills. I used to try to put down pieces and do illegal moves, and I had the perfect excuse.

"Well, I'm the only one looking after a baby as well," I would say.

They used to joke and say I was trying to cheat, especially as Daniel was usually asleep most of the time!

Other times we would just get together in one of our

rooms and chat. This aspect of rehab was bearable, but we used to talk about what was going on around us. The four of us had all been affected physically by our relative illnesses; however, a lot of the other patients had been affected mentally. Sometimes they could be very angry or unpredictable. It was not uncommon to walk down the corridor and have to avoid missiles being thrown about; chairs, cups, bins etc. I found this terrifying, especially if I had Daniel with me. Also, both during the day and at night, the air in the hospital was blue with patients swearing and shouting abuse at the nurses and doctors when they became irritated! The F-word was used non-stop.

As the weeks went by, Julie was moved into Room 4 next to me. I got to know her a lot better. She had had a series of brain tumours over the previous ten years and had then suffered a stroke after an operation to remove one of the tumours. I thought she was very brave. She was always joking and laughing with the rest of our little group, despite her long-term illness.

She was looking forward to her brother's wedding, which was to take place later that summer. Consequently, we enjoyed sharing her excitement and experiences of shopping for an outfit. One of Linda's previous jobs had been as a make-up consultant in Kendals department store in Manchester. Because of this she offered to do Julie's make-up for the wedding. One afternoon we had a trial run in Julie's room. We had a real laugh as Julie was transformed and Linda gave her lots of useful tips.

As we were all getting slightly better, we were all now allowed home at weekends and, as part of our transition back into normal life, we were also allowed to take leave in the week if it was a special occasion. At every possible opportunity Julie used to take leave and go off to The Trafford Centre with her mum or future sister-in-law to shop for an outfit for the wedding. She went so often that we said she must have shares in the centre!

One early evening I heard Julie's voice shouting my name. Well, it was obviously a cry for help, but it seemed very distant. I went into her room to see what she wanted, only to find the room totally empty. I thought my mind was playing tricks on me and then I heard her voice again.

"Jane, I'm here in the toilet," she shouted this time.

I have said before that we had a toilet directly across the corridor from us. I walked over and pushed the door. Julie was sitting there in her wheelchair, but somehow her arms were all wrapped up in her T-shirt. I pulled the orange cord in the toilet to alert a nurse. When one came I explained what had happened, and when the nurse had helped Julie back to her room and had left, I went in to see her. She told me that she had been escorted to the loo by one of the nurses. She had then decided to get changed into her nightie. Her stroke had also affected her left side, so she had the same difficulties I experienced. She had been trying to take her T-shirt off and had somehow got it caught on her left shoulder, so she could not put her nightie on after all. She also could not reach the handle to unlock the door and wheel herself back to her room.

It was a funny story, so I ventured down to Linda's room to tell her. I was already in my pyjamas, my cream satin ones. Linda said that she had heard all the commotion and had wondered what was happening. She laughed when I told her about Julie's misfortune.

The next day at breakfast Julie told the daytime nurses that I was her heroine as I had rescued her from a dilemma. She said she was now going to call me her 'knight in cream satin.' Because of this Linda did not stop singing the Moody Blues song, 'Knights in White Satin,' all day long.

~

During the summer, all the patients were subjected to the disturbance caused by staff shortages due to holidays. Because of this the nurses were rushed off their feet. Daniel needed his bath and nobody was available. Julie offered to help me, as she had no therapies that morning. We decided that if we got someone to lift him in and out of the baby bath, with our two good arms between us, we could hold him, wash him and still be safe. At this point our Welsh OT lady came to see Julie and she lifted Daniel into the bath for us.

Julie had been told that she could never have children because of her health. She still adored babies and told me that Daniel was the most demure baby she had ever met. She thoroughly enjoyed him gurgling and splashing in the baby bath. She said she hadn't had this much fun in ages. We had planned to stay in touch and she told me that she would tell Daniel about this when he was eighteen!

~

On the Monday morning following the August Bank Holiday in 2001, I returned to the hospital after a heavenly long weekend at home. When I arrived back at Cherry Tree I was shocked to find that there had been a patient riot over the weekend and that there were no therapies at all that day, as the staff were fully extended with escapees and patients kicking off!

The white notice board that I usually checked on my way

past the reception, was totally blank and there were to be no therapy sessions until things had calmed down somewhat. The patients' behaviour really had thrown a spanner in the works! After this discovery, I started to feel very bitter and twisted. The therapy sessions were the one and only reason that I had to be domiciled in hospital away from my young family, so without those I just didn't see the point in staying in hospital at all and lost direction.

Month by Month

My time in Cherry Tree was six months in all, but it felt like a whole millennium, as the time dragged and I just really didn't want to be there. I had to fill a bed at night to be considered an 'in-patient' and be eligible to receive physiotherapy and all the other therapies during the daytime. It felt so unfair. I thought it would be better if I spent the nights at home with my family (Dom, our gorgeous new son and of course Emily, who was by now a beautiful, blonde, inquisitive two year old) and then just came in every day for my therapies, but it was not an option.

I have included an event for each month to demonstrate the time that passed; however, the rest of the time was total monotonous routine, routine in between my therapy sessions. I am the kind of person who when I am shown a routine to follow, within days I will know that schedule better than the person who set it. I then became frustrated when things didn't happen when they were supposed to, or on the odd occasion when therapists were late for appointment times. I had made the effort to be ready on time, so why couldn't they?

I had arrived at Cherry Tree on *April* Fool's Day. There was a lady who served the breakfasts there. She was called Miriam and was a really genuine person. She was the ward clerk and in addition did the tea trolley, usually twice a day. She would write the date on the whiteboard in the dining room every day and if it was a special day of note she would let us know. Within weeks it was St George's Day and she wrote the date and drew a dragon next to it. I wondered if April would ever turn into May and so on.

From the dining room window we could see several cherry trees. The blossom grew and I asked which came first, the trees or the hospital name? The nurses were unsure. Some children came and threw a ball and knocked the blossom off. When the flowers disappeared completely, I was still in hospital. I felt like there was a life going on outside the hospital and I was no longer a part of it.

Miriam was always bright and cheery, and she made breakfast times bearable for me. I was usually first there because I had to be ready for Daniel arriving, and we would chat until the others arrived. At around 8.30 a.m., when Dom and Emily arrived to drop Daniel off, she would make a big fuss of Emily and give her some bread and jam before she went off to nursery. She adored Daniel and said that if I ever needed any help with him, she would always be there for me.

～

It was *May* and practically the whole of the rehab centre had heard about my friend, Debi, who had just gone to Las Vegas to get married. I worked on a hand-made wedding card (predominantly using my left hand, and it actually turned out okay) and envelope in my occupational therapy session and told everyone how I was going to the evening reception over here in a few weeks time. I was also going to watch the wedding on a live link on the Internet when I went home on leave at the weekend. It was all very exciting and my favourite topic of conversation at the time.

I had a whole physiotherapy session dedicated to seeing if I could wear a pair of proper shoes for the evening reception. I had only ever worn trainers since my stroke and I couldn't even walk perfectly in those yet. After attempting to walk up and down the gym in them, we decided that I was not going to feel confident in proper shoes, as I kept falling over on my weak ankle. The pair I took in to the rehab centre had been the comfy ones I used to wear for work with my suits, the ones with the smallest heels that I possessed. I felt like I was going over on my ankle every time I took a step, so I decided that when I had chosen what I would wear, I would buy myself a new pair of shoes rather than try and deal with a broken ankle on top of my other injuries!

Trying to decide what to wear was an ordeal in itself. I had a few dresses in mind, but when I tried them on I either could not do up the fasteners on them with one good hand, or my shoulders looked like skin and bones with the small straps, as I had lost so much weight! I eventually chose a pink floral dress that I had bought for Julia's wedding a couple of years before. That time I had worn it with some high strappy sandals and a little pink cardigan. I decided to wear the little cardigan to cover up my bony shoulders, but had to have a shopping trip to buy some new flat shoes.

We went into Stockport the week before the reception and I bought a pair of flat ballet-style shoes. They had an elastic

JANE COUPES

strap, so I could get them on and off without any problem. They felt okay when I walked in them, so we had a result.

That weekend we went to Dom's mum and dad's for tea and watched the wedding on the Internet. It looked great fun. Debi looked gorgeous and as a surprise her dad had flown over to the States to give her away. I could tell even from the link that she was thrilled. Elvis came into the chapel and serenaded Debi and Owen, and he finished the ceremony off with the hit 'Viva Las Vegas'! Dom's dad and I laughed together while we watched it. When we went downstairs we told Dom and his mum about it. We were especially excited by Elvis's appearance and also the way the minister said in his American drawl to Owen:

"Sir, you may kiss your bride!"

A couple of weeks later it was time for the evening reception at home. The couple had put a lot of effort into keeping the Vegas theme going. They had an Elvis impersonator and also casino tables around the venue. The menu was also a Tex Mex theme and very unusual for a wedding buffet, but delicious all the same.

I had had a really tough week in the rehab centre and when the Saturday came I was exhausted. Dom was looking forward to it also, so he looked after the kids and sent me back to bed in the afternoon to rest, so we would not have to leave the reception too early that evening. Around 6 p.m. he came upstairs to wake me and I got really upset and a little hysterical.

"I just can't go!" I exclaimed.

I was just so shattered and it felt like a huge effort to get all dressed up. Although I looked okay in my outfit, I didn't feel as nice as I had when I had worn the dress before and, although the shoes were fine, they were a little big and I wasn't fully used to walking in them. Dom said it was a confidence thing and we would have a good time. He could hold my hand firmly when I was walking and when I needed the loo, he said he would get one of my friends to walk to the ladies' with me and help to hitch my dress up if I needed it. I had only ever worn joggers and sports tops since I had been ill and these always had to be for ease of comfort and practicality - how boring! Dad gave Dom and me a lift to the hotel, and this summons up a memory of how frail I looked now I was dressed in something other than my usual joggers and trainers hospital attire!

We arrived at the hotel and whilst we hovered in the lift I was still very apprehensive. When we got out and found the correct function room, Debi and Owen were there to greet us. I got a big hug from Debs, and Owen said that I was their special wedding guest! All the effort and tears had been worth it. Of course, I had always wanted to go to the wedding 'do', but the fear of the unknown hotel and unexpected situation was overwhelming. That was it. We were out without the children and we were going to have a great time. After all, it was the first ever time that we had been out together since Daniel's birth!

When I walked carefully down the stairs to the dance floor and tables, Debi's sister, Lisa, and her fiancé, Lee, were there. I gave them both a hug and Lisa said to me that when she had watched me walk down the stairs, it had sent a shiver up her spine and had said to Lee, 'Look at her, she is amazing.' Well, I nearly burst into tears there and then. It was an emotional evening anyway, but for my friends to tell me that I was doing well meant so much.

The evening was great in the end and I saw some of Debi's family and friends, whom I had not seen since I had been ill.

JANE COUPES

They were all really interested to know how I was getting on with my rehab and all said I looked well. The only quiet reflective moment I had was when all my girlfriends got up on the dance floor.

"I want to go and dance, but I feel silly," I told Dom.

My balance and rhythm were no good any more, so I didn't feel confident enough to get up there and even shuffle my feet about!

At this point you need to know that I had met Debi and Lisa and another friend, Emma, when I had split with my ex-boyfriend. I had met them through my friend, Julia, who I knew from college and through another mutual friend. We were all single and in our twenties at that time, and for a couple of years we just went out and partied, having a great time, along with no shortage of male attention! Part of this was going to a local nightclub every Friday night and dancing the night away. Dancing was usually a big part of us going out. Now I could not join in and really felt it.

Anyway, by the end of the evening I had had a few alcoholic drinks and as the DJ wound up the evening with the last dance, I turned to Lisa.

"It's your turn next and my goal is to get up and dance at your evening reception!"

I had four months or so to practise.

~

Every month or so, Dr Downton arranged a team meeting for each individual patient. My first one was some time during *May*. At the meeting, Dr Downton, plus all the therapists and your own designated nurse, attended. This was an opportunity for Dom, myself and our families to ask any questions that we wanted to address. The 64 million-dollar question was, how long would I have to stay in hospital? Some patients asked and others did not.

At meals if the other patients knew you had attended a team meeting they would say:

"Did you ask *the* question?"

It became a standing joke. The answer from the specialists was always:

"How long is a piece of string?"

Every case was individual. Basically, they could not commit to anything, which was perfectly understandable, but very frustrating when you wanted answers. I wanted to know if I was ever going to get my life back on track. At the team meeting it was decided that they would arrange a meeting with social services to see what assistance I would receive when I was finally discharged.

During one of these meetings, I have a very vivid memory of feeling quite brave and asking Dr Downton a hard-hitting question about my recovery, in particular in relation to whether I would drive again. I wasn't prepared for her reply, which knocked me for six!

"The likelihood is that with the extent of your injuries, you will never drive again, work in your previous capacity or walk again."

~

Now it's *June* and there are more celebrations to attend. My auntie and uncle are celebrating a special wedding anniversary with a garden party and my friend's twins are being christened on the same weekend. As if that wasn't enough to contend with, my friend Julia is having her little girl, Annie, christened too, on the same Sunday afternoon. Before I was ill this could have been a normal weekend for us. We have always worked hard and played hard, and there was always something going on in the family or with our friends.

Again I remember another tough week in the rehab centre, in fact they were all hard and very tiring, and I looked forward to weekends to recharge my very rundown batteries. It was obvious that I was not going to get much of a rest this weekend, and that slightly panicked me. The weeks in hospital dragged on without anything happening and I longed for some action. At weekends I felt like I was being sped off on a runaway train and I sometimes wanted to get off. If this was the pace of real life then I started to wonder if I should just give in and live in the rehab centre for ever and a day!

My own health visitor had been brilliant since my stroke. As we had just moved house, I had only met her on a couple of occasions before Daniel's birth. She was very supportive and easy to talk to, and she called to see me in hospital every few weeks. As I felt so vulnerable, she tried to fight my corner for me with social services, but was limited to what assistance she could offer. On a personal note, she helped me greatly and she gave me a crystal that represented courage. It obviously worked because, although I had numerous difficult times in hospital, I eventually got through it.

I felt that she helped me regain my self-esteem when she came to visit me. She often tried to make her visits coincide with the times I had Daniel with me. She would tell me what a good job I was doing in my part of raising him. She told me that he never took his eyes off me when I was talking. I was not convinced, but she gave me a newly found confidence that I could be a good mum to him, despite my injuries.

I was worried that Daniel had not bonded with me even though I clearly had with him.

"Wait a while and soon he will be all over you like a rash.

Little boys and their mummies have a very special relationship," Dom said.

As I type this, Daniel is now two and a half and although he is coming around a little, he is still predominantly a daddy's boy. I try not to take it personally, but it did hurt an awful lot.

It was around this time, that I gave Daniel his nickname or pet name of 'Daniel Spaniel.' We all started to call him by this name, all our family and his new aunties (the nurses). At the time I typed this little paragraph, Daniel was seven and his nickname still slips into use on the odd occasion!

~

During one of Sally's visits, we decided to go outside for a walk around the hospital grounds, as it was a beautiful *July* day. I recall telling Sally that I felt quite threatened by the other patients and their behaviour. She said it was a natural instinct for me to want to protect Daniel. Because of this reason, she arranged with Dr Downton that I should spend some time in 'the flat'.

'The flat' was a self-contained unit within the hospital grounds. It was completely separate from the main building and when you were in there you were responsible for the key. It was normally used for patients who were ready to go home and it was kind of a final check to ensure that they would be able to cope on their own.

I felt pleased when I was told that I would be spending the days in there with Daniel. The same arrangement was to continue with the nurses and I was to buzz for them when I needed to lift him. When I got there, I liked having my own space so much that I asked if I could stay there at night too. The nurses checked and Dr Downton said that I could use it indefinitely until the next patient was due to be discharged. Although I had instigated this step forward, I was still apprehensive about staying there at night all by myself. Of course Daniel would be long gone and safely back home with his daddy.

"You are still at quite an early stage in your recovery. This is your big chance to show them what you can do," Dom said to me on the first night I stayed there.

I knew I was quite lucky to be given this chance, as usually patients were only sent to the flat the week before their discharge date. It was only July and, although I had resigned myself to being at Cherry Tree until September, nobody had confirmed this was definite. Now as well as getting myself washed and dressed, I would have to do normal everyday things like preparing my own meals, washing up etc. This also meant that toast was back on the agenda, so it had to be a good thing.

The occupational therapists supplied me with milk, teabags, cereal and bread. Dom and I went shopping for some snacks, sandwich fillings, ready meals, quiches and salad stuff. I would then be self-sufficient for the first time since my stroke. The flat had a big room with a sofa, a bed, a television (a full size one) and some wardrobes in it. There was a small kitchen and a tiny bathroom with a defunct shower and a toilet in it. I found it a little bit of a hardship to move all my stuff over there. The nurses helped me and I piled up Daniel's empty pram and wheeled most of my stuff across there.

I found the flat a great experience. It was nice to take some time out from the madness in the hospital, so that I could try and sort my head out and refocus on what I wanted to achieve while I was there. I could brew up for my visitors and it felt more like normal life again. I still had to go over to the main building for some meals and all my therapies, and also for a shower or bath, so I still managed to keep in touch with my rehab friends. I kept threatening to have them all around to the flat and have a little wild party. Unfortunately, it never actually came to fruition, as it would have needed too much assistance from the nurses to wheel patients across etc.

The big disadvantage of being in the flat was that every morning precisely at 6 o'clock, the sound of the milkman woke me up. This was his time to deliver a crate of milk to the nearby hospital kitchens, and the tailgate on his truck was very noisy indeed.

Although the flat was a good experience for me, I still said to Dom that it could be quite a frightening ordeal for some people. In real life I did not live on my own and, although I always stayed on my own when Dom was away on a course or on business, at home I had an alarm on the house. I still have friends who invite their mums to stay if their husbands go away on business, so it was a good job I had been partially hardened to it.

During Sally's visits she would bring her scales and weigh Daniel. The nurses and I used to try and guess how much weight he had gained. It was always good. He was thriving and developing well, even though I wasn't. Since my stroke I have always remained adamant that despite how tough things have been for me, I am grateful that Daniel was not the one who was poorly.

Some time during that summer a few of the patients were discharged, or 'released' as we used to call it.

"When will it be my turn?" I kept asking.

There were people being discharged who I thought were much more poorly than me. When I say this I mean mentally. Some patients were discharged when they didn't even know what day it was, but their physical condition was a lot better than mine. I felt it was unfair, as I just wanted it to be me packing up my stuff and saying my goodbyes. I wanted my release date to come so badly that I would fish for comments from the nurses. Of course they did not know. They were very diplomatic and professional and said I was doing well and that Dr Downton would make her decision about me all in good time.

Although Dr Lewis had handed over my care to Dr Downton, he was still responsible for my heart condition and, subsequently, during 2001, I had to go back to Stepping Hill Hospital for regular checks.

On one such trip, I had to go back for an echocardiogram, which was another scan on my heart. My dad arranged to take me there. The staff nurse at Cherry Tree gave me a huge file of my hospital notes to take with me. As I sat in my wheelchair, I placed the heavy notes in my lap. While my dad was getting a ticket for the car park, I decided to have a sneaky look in them. I discovered a piece of paper that Dr Lewis had written to Dr Downton when he initially referred me to her. In the letter he had said I was 'a remarkable young lady'. This made me feel good.

Dr Lewis commented on the notes and said they were so extensive that they were his weight training for the day! When I saw him after I had had my echo scan, he made me feel as if I was doing really well in my recovery and he did a little celebratory dance when we discovered that the scan had showed my heart was virtually back to normal. This was fantastic news. I also asked him if I now had a heart condition, or if I could carry on as normal without worrying about my health. He told me that as long as I did everything in moderation I would be fine! He also said that now I could stop taking all the heart drugs and that back at Cherry Tree they would be able to step up my physiotherapy even more now that I almost had a clean bill of health!

He also came to visit me one evening at Cherry Tree. It was the quiz evening when he arrived, things had just got off to a start and instead of asking one of the nurses to take me out and back to my room, he waited for around half an hour (bearing in mind as a busy consultant this was his valuable free time!) until the quiz had finished and I had been awarded my prize. He was highly impressed and overwhelmingly enthusiastic when I showed him that I could walk slowly across my room. When he left, one of the nurses with whom he had been chatting about my progress said what a nice man he was, and I emphatically agreed.

JANE COUPES

The Final Furlong

Throughout all that summer, my confidence in caring for Daniel slowly grew. It was great to have him with me during the days most of the time. We really started to bond and for the first time I felt that he knew I was his mummy. When Dom used to drop him off in the morning, he would also leave Daniel's bag. This had all his bottles already made up for the day, a new set of clothes and a pad in which Dom wrote down about Daniel's care. He would write down the time of his last feed and if he had poohed, what time etc. I started to feel quite involved in Daniel's care. I still could not help thinking that it was not the same as the time I had with Emily as a baby. I still have fond memories of that time, despite the sleepless nights. That was one thing that I was missing out on by being in hospital; however, I desperately wanted to be at home taking my turn at waking up and feeding Dan in the middle of the night.

Sometimes when I was dressing Daniel, I would curse Dominic under my breath. It was even more difficult to dress my baby than myself. His buttons and poppers were tiny and needed manual dexterity, which I no longer had. I soon adapted and became a champion at doing poppers with one hand and tying nappy sacks using my teeth to do the knot. It seemed that Dom always chose an outfit with loads of obstacles, but Daniel always looked very well turned out.

Some of the nurses who assisted me looking after Daniel used to be tactful and let us have some time alone. Some did not, so while I was cooing and talking silly baby talk to Daniel, I felt as though I was being watched and that something was not right. At other times I was glad that somebody would whisk him away. These times were usually during physio sessions. If he played up at my allocated time, I felt a little resentful towards him. I wanted to tell him how I would never be able look after him by myself if I did not fully concentrate, do well and get everything I could out of my sessions.

One Monday morning the staff nurse told me that as I was doing so well in caring for Daniel, they were going to reduce the amount of assistance I needed. This news came as quite a shock and I was very afraid. The thought of being left alone with a baby who I could not physically lift to console, terrified me. I started to cry.

The staff nurse explained that they were not withdrawing the care completely, but instead of somebody being with me on a daily basis, I was just to press my buzzer when I needed help to manoeuvre Daniel from one place to another.

There were so many nurses/female family members involved in Daniel's care that I felt completely and utterly stifled. The female physiotherapists especially tried to help me to cuddle Daniel. It was my ultimate goal to pick up my son with both arms and cuddle him. This became quite an issue and something out of my reach, as Daniel was already a strapping baby boy who was growing faster than my arm was getting stronger. As I was left more for periods of time on my own with him, I became more confident and he became *my* baby again. I started to pick him up by myself and manoeuvre him out of his pram onto my bed etc. However, rather than being a motherly cuddle, it was more like a rugby tackle as I bundled him under my right arm, trying to support a little with my left arm wrapped around his bottom. I always put his safety first and paramount, and if I felt a little tired or weak, I would just buzz and ask the nurses to lift him on my behalf.

The new arrangement with less assistance from the nurses actually worked out better. I did not have to make polite conversation for long periods of time and I felt that I could finally have some quality time with my son. I tried to make the most of it. I would tickle him, blow raspberries on his bare tummy and sing him songs that Emily had probably already known by heart at his age.

My routine of bathing Daniel every day soon changed after this new arrangement had taken effect. Previously I had needed assistance with lifting Daniel in and out of the bath. I also needed someone to stay for the duration of the bath time, so that I could have help lifting his head out of the water etc. I could do all the other bits, i.e. washing, drying and shampooing his hair.

I have already said that Daniel was thriving, and one day he got so big for the baby bath that his big toe caught the plug and the water went absolutely everywhere. It was a good job Stewart, the only male nurse, was assisting on this occasion, because we had to rapidly rescue Daniel, and then he had to mop all over my flooded room. We decided that it was time to review this method of doing things.

~

When you are living an ordinary life, you always imagine that having your mortgage paid off would be the best feeling ever. During that summer, we decided to claim against our critical illness cover and we did have a favourable result. I recall the day Dom told me very well.

The nurses had arranged to take a few of the female patients in a minibus on a day's shopping trip to The Trafford Centre one Monday morning. I wasn't happy about potentially being seen out in my wheelchair, but didn't want to miss out on some retail therapy. As we loaded up the bus, I quietly told one of the nurses about our large cheque (a substantial amount, which was the sum left outstanding on our new house/mortgage at that time), and she joked with me.

"Well, lunch is on you then!"

I was actually able to buy Daniel, Emily and Dom a small gift each on this trip and that was a lovely satisfying feeling after a long drought of gift-buying.

On my next weekend trip home, we went to the Bramhall Branch of Barclays to pay in the cheque. Dom dropped me as close to the door as possible and I slowly limped up to the counter (this was before I had taken ownership of my left foot again!).

"That's a nice one," said the casher, who had been trained to notice large cheques and the potential for investments, just as I had in my cashiering days.

Little do you know, I thought to myself. Later, when telling our parents, I was in a flippant mood.

"That house on St John's Wood, it cost me an arm and a leg!"

It literally had!

～

My second team meeting was some time during *August*. I had been subjected to the chaos that staff holidays cause in the summer in the NHS, and during my meeting Dr Downton said that we were now at a point where we could start to make some firm plans about a discharge date and what help would be required. She said my time at Cherry Tree was coming to an end. I was ecstatic.

"I know I have been here too long now, as I am beginning to think I could run the place better myself," I said.

The words had just slipped out. She laughed and told me to send a copy of my CV to her when I was better! I hold her in great esteem for her input into my recovery and I think she knows that. She is highly acclaimed in her medical field. I had just been subjected to things that would annoy anyone. Now I know why they call poorly people 'patients.'

At this meeting it was also decided that at some point it would be beneficial for me to spend another week in the flat in order to double-check that I was ready for life in the outside world. As I had already spent a week there, I did not feel as apprehensive this time.

Another crucial meeting, this time with social services, was arranged during August. Dom took time off work to attend. My therapists also attended the meeting and I was a little bit nervous about the outcome.

I had always worked since being seventeen and had been lucky enough never to need any dealings with social services. When the lady turned up from social services, she encapsulated all my pre-conceived ideas. She wore tie-dyed dungarees and was very 'right on.' She was not forthcoming with any reasonable solutions and she irritated me by saying that my children were now 'at risk.' I have said before that my mental condition had not been affected too much by my stroke, but I was livid when she said this. I suppose she was right in that if the children fell over, I could not physically pick them up. Other than that there was no issue with their well-being.

Afterwards I walked into the staff office and Mike, the physiotherapist, was there. He asked how the meeting had gone.

"Not great, and if my left arm had worked properly, I would have been tempted to punch her in the teeth," I replied.

"We'll do some work on it in the next session then!"

When I told my dad he was angry too. He decided to fight my battle against social services on my behalf, as I was so vulnerable. For the first time in my life, I realised how unfair the system is. We got into a wrangle over budgets. They said that because the children were not ill, our case fell in between departments. The children and families department would not take on our case because the children were both fit and healthy. The adult section would not either because technically I could look after myself. I just needed help with my children and that was what was stopping me from being discharged from hospital. If I had been a negative person, they could have made me slightly resentful towards Emily and Daniel because of this. However, I tried to think that I was a bigger person than that and I tried not to dwell on it.

It was now around 20th August and time for our annual trip across the Pennines to York races. This has become the perfect excuse for a get-together with our friends in York. Dr Downton allowed me to have a day off from my rehab, Dom took a day off work, as always, and a handful of our friends from Stockport (mostly old friends from Harrytown!) headed over to watch some racing during Ebor Week. I was apprehensive this year about how I would cope with the noise levels and crowd, but wanted to embrace the social gathering. I was disappointed that I was very frail and for the first ever time I didn't get dressed up in race attire, but had to go in some new joggers and a new T-shirt - how disappointing!

Once we had met up with our York contingent, savoured hog roast baps or other lunch delights and a few drinks (non-alcoholic for me this year!), we studied the form and the races began. Before we all had children we used to stay over and make a night of it, but now with babysitting arrangements and commitments, we were free agents for the races and a meal out in York at night.

In the 3.10 p.m. race - The Juddemonte International stakes - I bet on a horse (probably because the horse's mane had a nice plait in it when I watched it parade the paddock, you can see how serious my betting is!), Sakhee (also picked because of the jockey, L Dettori).

"Why is L Dettori written on the race card?" I asked. "I thought his name is Frankie."

I later found out his full name is Lanfranco Dettori. Sakhee romped home and I had a very small windfall, nothing life-changing (I think I just about afforded a round of drinks!), but I was particularly interested in tapping into that triumphant feeling. It was the final furlong for me in my long and eventful rehabilitation and I wanted to practise how fantastic that 'winning post' feeling (or going home, in my case) was like!

~

The events of 11th September have already made history. It was also a landmark in my recovery.

On the evening of the tenth, I had spent the evening being

physically sick. It felt like I was having a huge surge of hormones. The next day I started my period for the first time since I had delivered Daniel. This was yet another big step and meant that my brain had recovered somewhat and was now sending correct messages to my body. I was physically drained because I had been up half the night being sick.

During the day I stayed in bed and for the first and only time did not attend my physiotherapy session, as I was too weak. Instead I stayed in bed and watched the events unfold on the television. My mum came to visit me and I was glad, as she brought me a bottle of Lucozade and some rich tea biscuits, which she had done every time I was sick since I had been a little girl. I told her that I was not going to attend any of my therapies that day, but that I was 'throwing a sick day.'

"I'm not sure if you can phone in sick when you are in hospital!" she said, laughing.

Julie was also sick in the next room, as there was a sickness bug going around the hospital. She was also watching the events unfold on television in her room. The difference was that she was shouting out the breaking news at the top of her voice.

"How is our American correspondent then?" I enquired, when I saw her later that afternoon.

I am sure everyone remembers where they were that day, but it was particularly poignant for me in a very different way!

The next day was Dom's birthday and we had arranged to go out, just the two of us. When my sister-in-law, Nicki, came to pick Daniel up at two thirty, she said I looked awful. I told her that if I could get through a day like that, the rest of the time should be comparatively easy.

Just when you think things can't really get any worse, it

JANE COUPES

transpired at this time that I had evidently fractured a tooth during Daniel's birth. After putting up with a dull toothache for most of the summer and making numerous trips to the dentist, they could not do any treatment, as I was still on the blood-thinning drug, Warfarin. They said if I had to have an extraction I would have to go to see a specialist dentist at Stepping Hill Hospital. Meanwhile, I had a hairline fracture in my tooth and this was agony at times, especially when I had hot and cold food and drinks. Yet again, I was frustrated that I was in hospital and no one could do anything for me, except give me painkillers to numb the pain.

One day the toothache got so bad that the doctors decided that they would give me something a little bit stronger than paracetamol. They gave me some cocodemol. After I took it I began to feel very drowsy and started to hallucinate again. As usual, my dad came to visit that night and we still walked around the car park to practise my walking, but I was stumbling and had to link my dad's arm the whole way around our little circuit. I decided that I would just stick with the toothache rather than completely hinder my progress in walking again!

We still went for our meal at TGI Friday's restaurant in Cheadle. It was nice to take some time out for ourselves. However, the meal was spoiled slightly because I was still suffering from ghastly toothache. During that meal, we had a discussion about our forthcoming holiday to Oasis (it was after all our first ever family holiday since Daniel had arrived). We had initially thought that I would be farther on in my recovery by now, but we decided that if we were going to enjoy Oasis fully, we should take some help with us.

We decided to invite Dom's mum and dad as they loved helping with the children. We also knew they enjoyed Oasis, as we had all taken Emily when she was eight months old. I agreed, as I had always got on very well with my in-laws. Since I had been ill this had just increased. They were very supportive in all my hospital traumas. They had both experienced dealing with ill health before, as Dom's dad had been diagnosed with bowel cancer when he was in his forties. Because of this they could easily put things into perspective for me. Dom's dad had been so seriously ill that when they named Dom's youngest brother they called him Vincent Christopher (after his dad), as things had been so touch and go.

We also decided at this meal that we would ask Dr Downton if I could be discharged two weeks after we went on holiday. This would mean that I would have a week away in the Lakes, then have my last week in hospital when I could say bye to my rehab friends and have a leaving 'do', and then I would be discharged from Cherry Tree for good. I said to Dom that I would rather finish my hospital stint before we went away, but he convinced me that the last week would be relatively easy, as we could have a pizza night for my leaving 'do' and I could say bye to all the staff as well as the patients.

I had my third team meeting around this time, and during that meeting we discussed firm and final plans for my return home. Dr Downton said she would set up a meeting with the STAR team (Stockport Team for Adult Rehabilitation) and they would be my main source of contact for physiotherapy and occupational therapy when I got home. I had very high expectations of this team and was looking forward to working with them once I was finally settled at home. A final home visit was also organised. The hospital staff had already checked out my house for weekend visits, but they just

JANE COUPES

checked that I could go up and down the stairs etc., without any additional help, i.e. grab rails etc.

Dr Downton also confirmed my release date to Dom, me and both sets of parents, who were present at the meeting and who were also our backup for help when I was at home.

My second week in the flat was my last full week in hospital before we went on holiday to Oasis. Dom and I went shopping again to get some treats for meals while I was self-sufficient. This time in the flat I felt as if my vision had improved. I think I mentioned last time that the flat was near the gates of the hospital and was a great point for watching people coming and going. Before, the people had been bodies that went by in a dark shadowy blur, but this time I could make out faces and I could actually wave to the nurses as they strolled into the grounds to start their shifts. I also felt that I was more aware of my surroundings. I, therefore, convinced myself that my vision had slightly improved since the last time I was domiciled in 'the flat'!

My girlfriends had still continued their weekly visits on a Wednesday evening. This time I could make them drinks and arrange for Dom to bring Scooby snacks in for us.

At this point in my recovery, I was still going home every weekend and also during the week I was allowed home to my parents for tea. My dad would collect me and we would walk back to my mum and dad's house, which we measured at just over a mile away. This was a huge achievement in itself. The shower in the flat was still not working, so every Wednesday I would walk home with Dad and then Mum would help me have a bath.

"I bet you never thought you would be helping me to wash my hair at age thirty-two," I once said to her, and she acknowledged that it was a strange situation, but she was happy to do it.

At this stage I was completely unaware and oblivious that I was about to have my final hospital panic attack. My final stretch (which in essence was my second stint in the flat) was about to produce a huge wobbler!

PART FOUR
BACK FROM HELL

The Great Escape

On this, my second and final stay in the flat, I had the most horrible anxiety attack so far. Again I was doing really well at coping by myself, but this time I missed my rehab friends more. I felt a bit isolated, as I only went across to the hospital for therapies and then I wasn't always able to catch up with my friends because of different therapy times. I suppose the relationships I had built were stronger by this time.

~

One balmy summer night in September, I went straight to bed after Dom had visited me. Checking my arm and leg splints were on correctly and that I had locked the flat door properly, he then left to drive the now very familiar route back to our comfortable family home and our children, who were being looked after by another family member until Dom returned after visiting me. Meanwhile, I switched all the lights off and settled down to sleep really quickly, shutting out the fact that yet again I was in a strange bed.

I awoke at around midnight and realised that I had left

the television on. There was a nondescript American movie showing about a flood in a small town, and as I couldn't get back to sleep, I started to watch it in an absent-minded kind of way. However, there were things on my mind. I really was within reach of going home now and I was so excited I felt sick. I was also inwardly worried and a little apprehensive, as I had no idea what my new life at home was going to be like; however, there was a huge feeling of anticipation and also impatience (like when you have been successful in obtaining a new job and you're itching to get started)!

For some bizarre reason, however, I had another massive panic attack that night and I became totally irrational. I thought even though I only had two weeks left in hospital (and this was broken up by a week away in Penrith), I just couldn't take any more. Even this steely lady has a cracking point!

It was pitch black that night, but my mind started working overtime. I am physically close enough to home now that I could attempt to pack up all my belongings and walk home tonight, I thought.

As an aside now, I need to tell you that I have always been prone to getting carried away with things and blowing situations out of all proportion. Since I have been with Dom he is my person who brings me back down to earth and stops me from getting completely carried away. At this point in time I could not ring him, so called upon my inner voice to rationalise (I hope everyone has an inner voice like me, or I will be portrayed as completely bonkers!) and reel myself in, so, therefore, decided that I couldn't just turn up at home in the middle of the night, as I would wake Dom and the kids. Anyway, I didn't have a house key or any money. Offerton was not the best suburb to walk through at that time of night

JANE COUPES

and I was not quite physically up to the walk, even though it was just over a mile to our house. It would probably take me until morning to get home because of the number of stops I would need, so I decided to stay put and eventually went back to sleep.

I must have eventually drifted back into slumber and when I woke up the next morning, I could not believe that I had been contemplating escaping like a vagabond in the middle of the night!

~

My last home visit was later that week and I had progressed so much during my weekend home visits that the occupational therapist decided that the only extra provision I would need was a shower stool to help me at home because of the balance issues (or lack of balance) I had. The stool was a white plastic contraption, with a slanted seat with holes in and four sturdy metal legs. When I showered at the weekends, Dom would come in with me and help, minus the stool (and totally relish this opportunity!), but he couldn't do this on workdays because of time pressures, so I would need to be completely independent, hence I would need to shower sitting down.

We have a friend in York (Dom's best man, Dave) who is a complete practical joker, and when we had moved into the house he had arranged for us to be bombarded with junk mail via *Readers Digest*. At that time we had received lots of Saga holiday information and also that about hearing aids, stair lifts, bath chairs etc. It made me laugh (but also quietly and sadly reflect) that now I might actually be eligible to have some of these products in my house and at the age of only thirty-two. Deep down I just thought, I'm too young for all this to happen. There was also a part of me that didn't like having any aides in my house on loan from the hospital. They did not match anything and were not particularly attractive to look at, but they were there to help me, so yet again I had to bite my lip and have them in my bathroom and kitchen.

When Dom and I had showered together before my stroke, things had been hot and steamy, but now it was unfortunately supposed to be purely a practical thing and very boring, but nevertheless it was the physical contact that had been lacking in our relationship (for the first time ever since I had been incarcerated in hospital). Although now able to shower by myself aided by the shower stool during the week, Dom had seen how unsteady I could be and was still hugely paranoid about me falling over. I, therefore, started to ring him at work before and after I had showered, so that he knew I was safe and well.

It was around this time that we first received notification that social services had come up with a result and would in fact provide some help throughout the day to enable me to look after Emily and Daniel.

~

After spending a long hot summer inside (although sometimes cold and shivery for me now my blood was being diluted by the drug, Warfarin!), it was now time to get ready for Oasis (now Center Parcs). Altering our booking so that Dom's mum and dad were coming with us, the grand plan was that we would share a three bedroom lodge, and Margaret and Vincent would have one double room, with Daniel and his cot in it. Dom and I had the other double room and Emily had the room next to ours. Margaret did a lot of the organising in terms of the food we took for ourselves, i.e. snacks for breakfast and lunchtimes. It felt strange not to be the one

JANE COUPES

running around shopping and making last minute arrangements, but at that stage in my recovery I just couldn't have taken it on.

We set off on the journey, and I slept virtually all the way. Travelling any real distance, even though I was just a passenger and unable to share the driving now, was very tiring and something I had not done for a while. We stopped off in Penrith for some lunch. On previous trips to Oasis we had found a nice little pub that served good, cheap wholesome food, so we had a return visit there. The food was exquisite and tasted delicious to me after having hospital food for over six months.

We soon slipped into holiday mode and had a very relaxing week staying in a wooden lodge surrounded by acres of beautiful forest. As Daniel was sharing a room with his grandparents, Dom and I were even lucky enough to enjoy a couple of lie-ins. We did lots of walking. The air is so fresh up there you can almost taste it. On this occasion we didn't hire bikes, as I was not sure what my balance would be like and I did not want to risk another head injury. We took the children swimming to the pool every day and, although it was tiring, it was great fun.

Margaret and I also did some browsing in the many gift shops on site and as it was our break before I went back to hospital to say goodbye to my rehab friends, I bought them all a small farewell gift. I found some small teddy bears full of beans. They had names embroidered on their tummies, so I bought one for Julie and Linda. Attached to the bears on their ears was a plastic label and on this were listed attributes and traits associated with the particular name of the bear. I had a quick read of them and they did appear to be true from my short-lived experience of knowing my friends.

After this I nicknamed my friend and neighbour, 'Julie the Brave.'

As the holiday was nearing an end, one bright, crisp sunny morning I said to Dominic:

"Will you come with me around the lake?"

I wanted to prove to myself that I could walk the whole way around. We asked Dom's mum and dad to have the kids for a while and we walked *hand in hand* around the lake. I found it hysterical that we almost had to sneak off in order to complete this goal of mine. When we had been to Oasis on a previous occasion with my in-laws several years before Daniel's existence, we had made sure Emily was safe with them and had sloped off to have a dangerous liaison in the changing rooms. Now we were sloping off to practise my walking. How my life has changed! Anyway, when I got the entire distance around the lake I burst into tears. The scenery was beautiful and breathtaking, I was physically exhausted, so that probably added to the emotion, but I had done it, my next goal was complete. Life was good despite my difficulties and frustrations. I never thought something so simple could bring me so much joy. What a great feeling!

There was also a small disappointment on the trip. Although we took the children swimming every day and I got changed into my costume (an ordeal in itself with straps to trip me up while I was trying to balance on one leg in a confined cubicle!), I soon discovered that I could no longer swim. I had been quite a strong swimmer before, so this was very upsetting. I had hoped that swimming might be one of those automatic responses that Mike, my physiotherapist, had talked about, and I told Dom that when we got back home and back to hospital that I was going to pursue the possibility of going to hydrotherapy. I knew that some of the

JANE COUPES

patients already went to a pool in a nearby hospital, so I decided that swimming again soon would be one of my next goals to tackle.

~

I thought that the events of my final day in hospital, 26th September, 2001 (my release date!), would eternally be etched in my brain. However, as I write this there are bits that are still prominent memories - especially the elation and strong feelings at being set free, and the thrill and anticipation of being able to start to live a near normal life again. I can only compare that feeling to a scene in one of my favourite films, *The Great Escape* - hence the name of the chapter; do you see what I did there? I felt the same as I imagine Steve McQueen's character must have felt during his motorbike chase, after just escaping from the Stalag Luft III prisoner of war camp. However, there was also the feeling like when you pass your driving test (first time for me, I might add) that you really are only beginning to learn; there is lots of apprehension and still the most gigantic learning curve ahead.

I have now included a copy of a letter that I gave to the nurses (along with a huge box of chocolates) on my last day. I hope it demonstrates how grateful I was to all the nurses, who had given me superb care during my time there. I hope it also demonstrates how thrilled, excited and relieved I was to be finally set free from the rehabilitation centre.

I quite liked the sound of Dr Lewis' nickname for me, 'Little Miss Determined', so by now I decided I had the grounds to officially adopt it as my own!

To all the staff at DCNR
I feel I am about to disembark from the Rehabilitation

Rollercoaster at Cherry Tree Studios. There have been numerous ups and downs and difficult corners to overcome, but I feel I am now in with a chance of winning the prize at the end of the ride - a happy life with my family.

When I was on a peak day I felt very privileged to be a patient at the Devonshire Centre for Neuro Rehabilitation and on the trough days I was glad to have friendly faces about. I want to especially thank everyone who helped me around Anxiety Corner and various Hormonal Corners!

Thank you...
To all Dan's new aunties.

For treating me as Jane Coupes - an individual - and not Jane Coupes, stroke patient.

To Juliet, for arranging for me to bond with Daniel Spaniel.

To the Multisensory Room - 'my safe haven' - when the going gets tough, Jane goes to the MS Room.

To all the other patients, who are brave warriors trying to regain ownership of their lives in a world without toast.

Jane Coupes
aka Little Miss Determined

Thank you for looking after our mummy.

My two little rascals

~

I remember Dom's mum and his youngest brother and sister, who were both students at the time, came to help me pack my stuff up and I took great satisfaction in looking back at the empty room, now without Daniel's and my personal belongings. I wondered who the next unlucky occupant would be and walked off for the last time with a big crooked smile on my face. When I got home there was a huge bunch of flowers on the doorstep that my rehab friends had arranged to be delivered and loads of balloons around the front door.

~

In the early days following my return home, I found it quite difficult to adjust to my new life. Whilst in hospital, stupidly, my assumption had been that once I returned to my own home my left arm would work again and I would be able to do all the things I had done before and just slip back into pre-stroke life, except that life now included Daniel... I found it really hard when I woke up every morning, and for ages my first thought was, I still can't move my arm yet. Dom told me not to dwell on it and that my home visits from the physiotherapists and occupational therapy staff on the STAR team would start soon then I could continue progressing.

During those early days, we also had to address what had happened. Dom told me in detail about the events when I had my stroke and he showed me our phone bill, (which was with lots of other paperwork that Dom had dealt with, but not filed away) which was itemised with numbers and call times etc. He showed me all the calls he had made whilst I had been on the HDU; all early morning calls to check I was well and had in fact survived the night.

"Look, on this particular day you didn't care about me that much because you couldn't be bothered ringing until 9 o'clock," I joked.

It was all in jest and he knew that, but we had a deep conversation about the fact that I could very easily have not

JANE COUPES

made it, and there were lots of conversations that we had never got around to having, like which school we wanted the children to go to, we never did send those forms off to make our will etc. I got really upset and started sobbing. It just wouldn't stop. I felt like I needed to watch a sad film and sob all the way through, and virtually destroy a rainforest of tissues for it to be even slightly better.

In typical woman fashion, I also started to torture myself with lots of 'what ifs?'. I thought about Dom as a young widower, the thought of him with someone else, also who would have helped Dom raise our children and would they have done a good job and considered my high standards and values? The thoughts of these scenarios churn my stomach, make tears well up in my eyes and my face becomes contorted at this precise moment, but they are academic anyway, as I wouldn't have been around!

We felt a need to joke about it, but it really wasn't funny. Dom and I have had to use our spookily similar sense of humour to lighten moments and almost shut out the tragic and seriously life changing events that have happened to us.

Dom also relayed to me a conversation that he had had with my dad on the night when I had survived my stroke.

"Think about all the feelings you have for Emily," Dad said to him. "Well, Jane is my Emily!"

At the conception of my new life, I felt as though I had no role any more. Now when I came downstairs, I automatically went to put the kettle on and then open the curtains near the patio door, but now there was a two-year-old little girl already trained to do her best to open them. Our laundry was being shipped out between both mums. Our dads were on top of mowing the grass and tidying the garden etc. Sounds perfect, you may think, until you are in that situation and feel totally and utterly useless, but unable to change it. There were lots of arrangements being made in which I was no longer included. I think on my first low day since leaving hospital I said:

"You would all prefer it if I had in fact died!"

In those first few months we were advised that I could now claim disability living allowance, as I was no longer able to work. Dom tried to go through the forms with me and I told him that I was totally freaked out that I was even eligible for it. I feel as though I have always had a fairly healthy attitude towards disabled people; however, suddenly when it's you they are talking about, it feels peculiar. Since that time, I prefer to think of myself as a work in progress. I am someone trying their utmost to get the best possible recovery they can.

All of our extra help could not continue indefinitely. Dominic and I had made an executive decision that as I would be unable to look after Daniel and Emily by myself for a long time, we would change and extend the days the children were in nursery to three days a week, Tuesdays, Thursdays and Fridays, and also put Daniel into the same fantastic nursery that I had chosen when I had returned to work after having Emily. It then seemed realistic for me to look after the children (with help that was to be provided by social services), two days per week, Mondays and Wednesdays. This would also enable me to have three days a week to myself, which would be dedicated to my physical recovery (including necessary rests to allow my heart to repair), so that I could eventually and gradually build up the time I was able to have my children at home with me.

I felt a little sad that Daniel was only eight months old when he started full days in nursery; however, Emily had

JANE COUPES

been nine months when I had returned to work part-time, in fact two days, and if I had been able to revert back to the original plan, Daniel would have been in nursery part-time soon anyway, when I went back to work.

A few weeks after my return home, I started by borrowing an exercise bike from Dom's Auntie Terry. I would allocate myself a time when I could go upstairs and cycle whilst listening to one of my compact discs. At first I could keep pedalling for a couple of tracks and then I gradually built the time up, until I could cycle very gently until a whole compact disc had played. With two young children, obviously I needed the time and freedom to do this, so the days when they were in nursery seemed the natural choice, therefore, I started to do this every Tuesday and Thursday, and then I began hydrotherapy sessions on a Friday morning at the pool over the fence from our house.

Virtually housebound, as I couldn't walk far, I had to revert to a very different lifestyle; one that felt very lonely to begin with after my previous very active life. The possibility of going out, stumbling and risking another head injury was too great, so I had to completely re-evaluate things. I was unable to venture out even to post a letter, as the nearest postbox was across a busy main road and I was no longer quick enough to dodge the traffic! I had no commitments except plenty of doctor's appointments, the odd appointment for physiotherapy or occupational therapy, and these were at home anyway, as the STAR team travelled around making house calls. My friends had mostly returned to work after having their children (as in my original plan), so I couldn't really contact them during the daytime. I desperately needed some guidance/direction.

I remember feeling very excited when I had a hospital appointment with one of my three different consultants. This meant that my dad would pick me up and give me a lift to the hospital; it meant I could see trees, traffic and the outside world for a change and, although I relished this, I was still always glad to get back to the safe zone of my own home.

Before my physiotherapy and OT appointments with the STAR team began, I recall one morning when Dom and the children had gone off to work/nursery. I made all the beds and then needed to lie down again, as I had used up all my energy just by showering, washing and dressing. I wandered downstairs for breakfast and then recall thinking that the post was late. Around lunchtime it still hadn't arrived and I remember contemplating ringing the post office to complain. Get a grip, Jane, you are thirty-two and have more to worry about than what time the post arrives, were the words my inner voice said to me! When you are stripped of all your responsibilities/commitments, you start to think about completely trivial things!

This was also the day when I got back into reading books properly. I had the very first Harry Potter book on our bookshelf, but up until now I had felt too unwell or been unable to concentrate for long periods of time to follow a storyline/plot.

After my afternoon rest, I started to read it and had set myself a target of a whole chapter without my concentration wandering; however, in reality I read virtually the whole book of *Harry Potter and the Philosopher's Stone*. I was addicted to reading again and this was a truly great feeling and meant that my little world of escape was back! I did mean to write to J K Rowling to thank her, but from that point on life started to get busier and normality started to take shape again. Thank heavens!

JANE COUPES

As far as my swimming goal goes, I decided to begin by prompting the STAR team to send me to hydrotherapy sessions near our house. The sessions were in a pool attached to Offerton Centre for Learning Disabilities, which was literally over our garden fence at the side of our house. Hydrotherapy was a surreal experience. It was like bathing in a very hot bath, only there were other people trespassing in your bath. The ceilings were very high, so the echoes and sounds reverberated around the pool area and the heat made me feel quite bothered. However, once actually in the pool, my muscles automatically relaxed and I felt as though I might be able to get some movement from my left arm and leg.

During these Friday sessions there were lots of young disabled children having sessions too and as it was the highlight of their week, all the staff sang songs, usually 'Old McDonald had a Farm'! As the weeks progressed I developed and could soon swim a length of the pool using a swimming aide they called a 'noodle' because of its shape. I thoroughly enjoyed the sessions and worked hard to expand on the number of lengths I could achieve. When I got to 40 lengths during one session, they decided I was too good and my hydrotherapy sessions came to an end. However, I still couldn't get my left arm to join in no matter how much I willed it to join in and do breaststroke arms.

～

A certain type of behaviour that happens after a stroke became apparent during this time and this was an obsessive compulsive trait. I had already shown inklings of this throughout my life, so for a while things went a bit manic. This behaviour is a control thing and is a symptom of the stress/trauma that your body and mind have suffered. It started by me trying to help out with small jobs around the house that I could do to assist Dom in caring for our children. I would get their clothes out for the following day and lay them neatly on the sofa. The trouble is I would start to do this almost as soon as they had left each morning! Dom used to joke with me and say that one day he would come home and the entire contents of the children's wardrobes would be neatly placed in piles, almost enough for two weeks worth of wear!

Over this time I was gradually improving all the time. The progress was so slow and slight that I could not see any rewards; however, people who I only saw from time to time were always quick to say that I looked really well. My recovery slowed down somewhat and reached a plateau, but I was in fact still moving in the right direction.

Progression,
Progression,
Progression

Sometimes a progression was something so trivial like me being able to grip the side of my kitchen waste bin with my left hand, long enough to start putting the liner in with my good hand. Rather than go through every minor triumph, I have decided to write about the major ones that happened over the following years.

~

From my release date in September 2001 to the end of that eventful year, I unintentionally became a bit of a recluse, as I was so unnerved and anxious about going out into the real busy world that now seemed to go at such a fast pace after time had virtually stood still for me whilst in hospital. It didn't mean that I didn't want to be part of that world again soon, and I became quite irritated when the STAR team started to visit, and would be very impressed and comment favourably when I could answer the doorbell in quite a short space of time. I guess they were used to calling at houses where people were still wheelchair bound and took some time to get about.

I felt that I was marked and that they couldn't wait to get me off their patient list, so that they could help in caring for someone who wasn't as mobile as me. I felt that I was almost a victim of my own rapid success. For me, yes, it was great to be able to answer my own front door, but there was also a whole wide world out there that I wanted to explore again very soon!

The STAR team certainly didn't live up to my very high expectations. When in hospital the nurses told me that they would help me with everyday tasks like hanging washing out and basic chores, so that I could then be independent and, although they did provide a few small solutions for me, the team was totally under-resourced and often the stretched staff struggled to keep appointments. The physiotherapists on the team all seemed very young and inexperienced, and there was obviously no retention in that role, consequently, the staff turnover was very high and I felt there was no continuity in my treatment, as the newly qualified students went off to explore new horizons, and who could blame them? At one point I was actually given bad guidance and told to stop doing one of my crucial weight-bearing exercises with my left arm! I was so vulnerable and they were supposed to be the experts, so I was in a total dilemma.

For a while all our shopping was done via the Internet. I only ventured out at weekends when I felt secure with Dom and then, if it was a long trip, I was still reliant on my wheelchair, which I had secret plans to ditch very soon. On those trips out I did experience the negative publicity that goes with being in a wheelchair, when people would ask Dom questions on my behalf and blatantly ignore my wishes. Those trips had to be planned to military precision, as in the wheelchair scenario you have to check routes for suitability, i.e. any inclines in surfaces, kerbs etc., and also ensure that there are wheelchair facilities at your destination.

~

My hopes were riding high as we drove down the M56 motorway heading to North Wales. It was 31st October, 2001, and we were heading towards the North Wales Disabled Drivers Assessment Centre, based in Glan Clwyd Hospital, for me to be assessed for driving and future mobility.

Deciding to make a day of it, my mum squashed in between Emily and Daniel's two booster car seats on the back seat of the car. Mum was to look after Emily and Daniel while I was being assessed. It was one of those clear, crisp, sunny autumn days, so we had a very pleasant drive to Wales. I sat in the front with Dom and watched him manoeuvre the controls of his Golf, and longed for it to be me driving again.

When we arrived I felt anxious and nervous, but Alex and his friendly team soon put me at ease and explained that they were there to do everything possible to help. I was shown around the centre and it reminded me of the character M's workshop in any James Bond film. There were dashboards with adaptations so innovative that I really did feel that I was in with a chance of a favourable outcome. There were black plastic balls on steering wheels, which meant you could steer the car just by using your right or strongest hand, and a magnitude of switches/buttons on the dashboard that were to operate the windscreen wipers, indicators etc. I even saw a car that had mechanics fitted, which could collapse and fold a wheelchair and then slot it underneath the car chassis. I had already worked up to a stage where I could now easily transfer into a car passenger seat, so felt I was a slight step ahead in that getting in a car wouldn't be a problem for me.

Mum read stories and played games with Emily and Daniel while my assessment began. I was given a sight test without the use of glasses. I have never worn glasses anyway, so this went well and seemed a positive start. I was then given a cognitive test, which I sailed through. One of the tasks was that I remember the man asking me to sort some coloured plastic shapes into piles. When I asked him if he would like me to sort them by shape or by colour, Dom smiled at me from the other side of the table and I knew I'd done well. However, he wasn't so positive when he saw my clock face with numbers that I had been asked to draw. I felt like I was doing my best, but struggled to keep the paper still while I drew with my pencil in my good hand. When I finally looked properly at the shaky, haphazardly drawn clock face with wonky numbers in all directions, I wanted the earth to swallow me up and I suddenly felt that my big chance was gone. I had so much (it felt like my total independence) riding on this assessment and now it wasn't looking good.

Next came the practical test in the assessment centre car park and at last I was able to have a go at using one of those vehicles with a black golf ball on the steering wheel. It felt great for me to be behind the wheel again and I felt confident and smiled at Dom, who waited in the centre as I tried to get used to the new way of steering. We drove around the car park and I listened carefully and carried out everything that the instructor required of me. We even ventured out of the centre and down a main road, only for a short distance, and then straight back into the car park, which was when it all went pear-shaped for me.

My instructor asked me to position the vehicle over the centre of some white arrows painted on the ground of the car park to ease traffic flow. Although I felt like it went reasonably, when he gave me his appraisal later, apparently I was always a little to the left of centre and this, coupled with the disastrous clock drawing, was enough evidence that my spatial awareness had been affected by my stroke and, therefore, driving was no longer an option. Well, you can imagine the tears flowed until we reached Llandudno and tucked into our fish and chip lunch in a small seaside café and then walked along the beach, this treat only slightly easing the disappointment. I can still feel the wretchedness and desolation like it was yesterday...

It felt like my world was shattered that day, and the outcome was that it was unsuitable and unsafe for me to drive, as I now had a visual defect in my left eye and also a lack of spatial awareness. I was distraught, as I had pinned so many hopes on the outcome. When you have been used to driving and then suddenly cannot, it feels like your world is closed down. It then becomes difficult to just call in and see your friends or family without booking a specific and sometimes costly journey in a taxi. Even then it can be difficult to stop off en route and run extra errands, as you tend to book a specific journey. I felt that if I had been forced to name the top five worst things about having a stroke, not being able to drive any more would have been my number one on every occasion!

~

In 2002 I joined a rehabilitation gym called Total Fitness in Wilmslow. I did some research and it seemed to be the best in the area, plus it had also been recommended to me by Anna, my physiotherapist at that time. She was a member there herself and told me it could be really positive for my recovery. She was a positive for the STAR team and I wished I had worked with her more often, but soon she left to explore new horizons too.

As it was quite a distance to Total Fitness, Dom took me to have a look around one weekend. We left the children with one set of parents, and a lady called Lesley showed us around. She was very aware of some of the difficulties I would face by joining a mainstream gym, but we devised ways that I could get by, i.e. I would use the steps from the foyer to get up into the gym, rather than the spiral staircase that wound up from the changing rooms and was not wide enough for my unsteady and clumsy feet.

The gym is built on old Ministry of Defence land and it is almost in the shape of an aircraft hangar. Inside there is a 200-metre running track that goes around the edge of a mezzanine floor. In the centre of the track is all the gym equipment. Downstairs there are changing rooms, the women's gym, two swimming pools and some little shop outlets. It is huge and like a little village in itself.

As I walked around the gym with Dom, I got a really positive vibe and almost a buzzing feeling. I looked up as we leaving and could envisage myself six months down the line confidently walking around that track and using some of the equipment.

Once we had crunched all the numbers and slept on it,

Dom and I decided that it could be something really positive into which to channel my depleted energy.

On my first visit there I had to have an induction with an instructor, which all new members need to do. I saw an instructor called Scott and, together with the advice of my physiotherapist, Anna, he soon devised a gentle programme for me. He wanted me to go on a treadmill and I had never attempted this before (even though I had had gym programmes in a previous life!), so was a little apprehensive. As I was learning to walk again, my steps were very slow and calculated, and I was worried that I might trip up and fall over as the momentum of the machine took over. Scott put it on the lowest speed setting possible and I stepped on and took it slowly. He talked me through my programme and wrote it on a card for me to follow. He also encouraged me to build on any speeds/times when I felt able to.

As I looked around the gym there were lots of men in there.

"There is a ladies only gym downstairs if you would feel more comfortable working out in there," Anna said.

"Blokes don't phase me!" I replied straightaway.

On my first solo trip to the gym, Mum and Dad drove me over to Wilmslow, and they called into Marks and Spencer at Handforth Dean to do some shopping while I completed my brand new programme. We agreed to meet a few hours later in the juice bar inside the gym. I went about my programme and only needed to ask for assistance once, as I could not adjust the seat height on the bike. I chose a treadmill in a quiet corner and managed to do ten minutes without any difficulty. I stopped to have a sip of water and looked down at the swimming pool, which looked very inviting now I was hot after a workout. This naturally became one of my next goals; to take the good work I had been doing at the hydro-therapy pool and transfer it to the pool in the gym.

At this stage getting dressed, folding clothes and fastening my bag up were still a problem, but I used my teeth to help where my left arm could not hold an item.

Consequently, my visit took longer than I had anticipated and when I got to the juice bar Mum and Dad were sitting drinking coffee and chatting to one of Dad's old friends and his wife whom they had bumped into. They introduced me to Anne and Jim, who had been regulars at the gym since it had opened, and this couple said that they would look after me if I ever needed any assistance with anything whilst there.

It had been a successful trip and I was fired up to do more. I felt great as I left the gym, but later on that afternoon the fatigue hit me and I was shattered after my physical exertions.

I soon became a regular at the gym on the days when Emily and Daniel were in nursery. This meant that every Tuesday and Thursday I got a taxi from our house in Offerton, followed my programme in the gym then got a taxi home to have a rest before Dom and the kids returned.

I quickly got to know a few people. There was a whole cross-section of people there, mostly retired people who wanted to do some gentle exercise, also the Sale Sharks rugby team used to train there and they were very driven to achieving peak fitness. Sometimes if I was next to one of the guys on the treadmill, it seemed very obvious to me that my programme was very gentle and they were going full pelt, so I would mutter under my breath.

"Not bad, but I guess we have very different goals."

I suppose them being there tapped into my competitive side and made me work all the harder. I think there was even a time when I tried to keep up with them whilst using a row-ing machine! It also meant that there was occasionally a bit of eye candy around to make the trips go faster!

On each visit after my hard work and when I had completed my programme, I went downstairs and used the sanarium, steam room and jacuzzi, as relaxation for my tired muscles. My instructor, Scott, had advised me to use the samarium, as it has a more gentle heat than the sauna. He also told me that I could use everything down there, but he really didn't advise me to use the cool option in the therapy showers with my heart condition.

Being my usual inquisitive self, I decided that instead of pressing the tropical rain button, one day I would try the cool rain button. A quick and fierce jet of icy cold water came out and soaked me through. I gasped out really loud. My left arm quickly folded itself into my body as an adverse reaction to the extreme cold and I struggled to catch my breath for a good few minutes. This was the only time since my recovery that I had not taken on board the advice given by the specialists, so decided that I would never do that again!

However, I found my many repetitive hours at the gym very empowering and felt great that I had so much input and effort into my recovery - this time I was starting to see the rewards!

Signing up and joining the gym was the easy task. I then had to find the motivation and energy to get there at least twice a week. This was particularly difficult, as now I was back at home, Daniel was disturbing our sleep during the night on a regular basis. I just equated this problem to the time when I returned to work after having Emily. My physical recovery now had to be considered my work and I just had to get on with it as if I had returned to work and still had a commitment to be there. The only times I ever missed a session were if Emily or Daniel was ill and unable to attend nursery then I had to be a mum first and foremost.

As I see it, my membership of the gym was one of nine major things that happened during that year in terms of my recovery.

The second thing was that finally, after a long battle, social services came up trumps and decided they would fund someone to come and help me in my own home to look after my children at long last. This had been ongoing since our initial meeting with them whilst I was still in Cherry Tree. My dad phoned and dealt with more than a dozen people, getting nowhere. Having eventually found the director of social services' direct number (for the phone on her desk) he rang her. She was initially more interested to know how Dad got her telephone number than helping me, but this soon changed.

We decided to start with the two days when the children were not in private nursery, Mondays and Wednesdays, and gradually build the time up. I really was not looking forward to having someone intruding in my house with my family, but it was the only way I could do what I wanted, which was to have just me looking after my own children whilst Dom went to work.

The first person they provided I shall call Karen. She was a young girl in her twenties and, although she was good with the children, she brought lots of issues with her to work. She was forever having arguments with her boyfriend, which affected her attitude to work, she was often late just when something critical had been needed for the children, which meant that if she had not arrived, Dom could not get off to work on time, and she made herself a bit too comfy in my house. When I walked out of a room, she would switch over the television from the CBeebies channel (that Emily and

JANE COUPES

Daniel had been watching) to whatever she fancied watching, and I felt she took advantage of the fact that we provided lunch for her. The only positive was that she had a car and would take us out to the park or to an adventure play area from time to time; however, I honestly felt that this was what she was being paid to do.

The crux came when she came in to work and complained that she felt unwell because she had been out the night before for a curry and some beers. She was really there to do the physical things like carrying Daniel, opening jars of baby food, carrying washing baskets around the house and anything I could not do myself, so when she offered to carry Daniel upstairs to his cot for an afternoon sleep after I had given him lunch, I thought nothing of it. She was gone a while, so I edged my way slowly up the stairs to see where they had gone, only to find that she was almost laying next to Daniel on our double bed in our bedroom! I was livid, so immediately rang Dom at work. He told me that her behaviour was unacceptable, but I really shouldn't do anything rash, as I could be shooting myself in the foot. He said that if we caused any unrest, social services could just withdraw the help and we would be back to square one.

Throughout our relationship, I have always been able to rely on Dom to calm me down and make me think before I steam in and upset the apple cart. He was right on this occasion and, although we said we were going to speak to someone, the situation dissolved itself when Karen came in the following week and announced that she had found another job. I was so relieved, but when I sounded out my friend, Michelle, about it, she quite rightly told me that it could actually have been anyone helping me out and I would have had a problem with them. I did actually quite like the girl after all. In a work environment, I had always been marked really high at appraisal times on managing relationships, but when it is in your own home and involving your own children, it is a whole different issue to deal with. There is a very fine line between helping and interfering, whether by social services or family!

The next lady they provided, whom I shall call, Yvette, was much more suitable. She had a child of her own and even though she had to travel quite a distance to our house, was much more reliable. However, this only lasted a short time as any funding was only agreed on a short timescale.

~

We also finally arranged to have Daniel christened in 2002. With all the problems that had been going on, it had never occurred to us about getting him baptised. We got my dad to ask the priest at his church, St Joseph's in Stockport, to christen Daniel, as we had never been to church in our new parish, having been focused on other things. Once we had a date, Dom sorted out the venue for the celebrations afterwards, The Moorfield Arms in Mellor. We ploughed through the menu options and Dom enjoyed me sending him up there to advise them of our final choices. Any excuse for a quick pint! Our choices were an exquisite sausage and caramelised onion casserole, lasagne, chicken curry and then a feast for the many children present.

We made a list of all the people we wanted to invite and we even included a few of my rehab friends and Brenda, my favourite nurse from when I had been in hospital. She had been so supportive to me throughout my time in hospital and she had also given Daniel lots of cuddles and fussed him in a way that I couldn't, as I was too ill.

During the church service I remember feeling a little hypocritical as we were all joined in prayer thanking God for the arrival of this wonderful baby. These were my sentiments too, but there was also a small feeling that, although I loved my baby boy heaps and had always done so since his birth, I just felt that his arrival had been too costly to my own health and had changed my life so dramatically that I felt a little unsure as to my true feelings. Look, see I've just typed it in black and white and, therefore, admitted it. In true therapy style - my name is Jane Coupes and at one point in our relationship I was not sure whether I loved my son or not!

At that moment, I made a conscious decision that he was my son and together we could be bigger and our love could be more powerful than this horrible scenario that had been sent to test us. Even though at the point of Daniel's christening, our relationship was not the way I wanted it to be, I secretly knew that if we worked at it we would get there in the end.

On that day he looked so handsome and gorgeous. Dressed in a white sailor suit with navy stripes, borrowed from his cousin, Joshua, and then passed back for his younger brother, Cameron, he really was the star of the day. His then blond hair was quite long and he even had a fringe, something he would not tolerate now. He had just turned one and started to walk, and at The Moorfield Arms afterwards, he showed off his new walking skills to all our guests and totally relished the moment. Our other star of the day was Emily, dressed in a pink dress and cerise cardigan, with a matching floppy hat, and if you were seated at the back of the church, all you could see was a little pink hat bobbing around above the church benches. She really did derive pleasure from spending that day with all her young cousins.

I just wanted that bond with Daniel like I used to have

with Emily. She always came to me first when something troubled her, and still does, but Daniel always diverted to Dom first and probably any other grown-up who was around before coming to me, which was really quite damaging, but if I'm totally honest, often I was so poorly/tired I was glad that he didn't bother me when he needed something! I hated the way when he woke in the middle of the night, it was always Dom who had to go and physically get him, and when he could walk, he naturally walked straight past my side of the bed, nearest the door, and around to Dom for some comfort.

~

In the summer, Manchester hosted the Commonwealth Games and Dom had sent off for tickets well in advance. We went to watch on the middle Sunday afternoon of the games, 28th July. My mum and dad came to baby-sit the children and we had asked our friends, Trevor and Caroline, to join us, as Dom had a couple of spare tickets. They only lived around the corner at the time, so we walked around to their house. Trevor's dad gave us a lift and dropped us off near The City of Manchester Stadium.

There was a fantastic buzz around the crowd sitting outside the ground and it was totally civilised as we sat having drinks in the sunshine. When we entered the ground and found our seats, Trevor tried to ring some of our other friends, who we knew were also attending that evening.

"Wave your hands about, so we can see you," he said, speaking on his mobile phone.

We looked around the crowded stadium and, although the seats were mostly full, we could not pick out our friends, Bernard and Lorna, from the masses. Suddenly there was a

JANE COUPES

bit of a stir around us and it was such a lovely friendly atmosphere that a complete stranger said:

"There they are, over there."

We looked over to the opposite stand and could see them waving at us like mad things.

On that early evening we were lucky enough to witness Jonathan Edwards win the triple jump final and Paula Radcliffe win the 5,000 metres final. She ran around the track really close to us and she looked so comfortable, even on her final lap she was smiling, which was another fillip for me. Although we had goals that were worlds apart, her performance gave me renewed inspiration to continue with my physiotherapy, gym trips and my quest for a full recovery!

~

It was coming up to 8th March, 2002. Oh no, one year to the day exactly since my stroke. How am I going to react? Will I get upset? Will I be looking back to that time when I was so poorly? Dom diverted me from these questions that year by planning a weekend away for just the two of us.

"You will need your passport, but I'm not telling you where we are going until we get to the airport," he said.

When I tried to quiz him, so I could plan my wardrobe for while we were away, he told me to just pack my bag as if we were going away in this country. I went on a shopping trip with Mum and bought a couple of items; however, at this time I was still really restricted to what clothes I could wear, as I had to always check fasteners to ensure that I could tackle them with my good hand. Eventually I got some stuff that was both stylish for a trip away, yet practical too.

When we arrived at Manchester Airport, Dom told me that our destination was Charles De Gaulle Airport, Paris. I was thrilled. Club class, no kids, was definitely the best way to travel on our trip. We stayed in a fantastic chic hotel near Notre Dame and during our trip we took in the Eiffel Tower and the Sacre Coeur, which I found so spiritual, and had to contain my emotions. We also visited one of the museums and the Arc de Triomphe.

"I want to go and have a look at the view from the top," Dom said to me. "I'm not sure you will be able to climb the steps, so you might be better waiting here for me."

No chance. I wasn't going to miss out on some great views of Paris, so proceeded to climb the 282 steps to the very top. Yes, when I got to the top I was quite breathless, but so were lots of other people, who didn't look like they had a heart condition like me! What a triumph for me! I was rewarded with some stunning views and afterwards we went shopping along the Avenue des Champs-Elysees and yes, the trip had worked, although we still had to pace everything we did and build in lots of rests for me. I totally forgot that it was my first anniversary of that awful day in 2001 when I had only just survived in order to see the wonderful things that I now thoroughly enjoyed and savoured.

~

During the May of 2002, we were able to successfully arrange holiday insurance for me for the first time since my stroke, so we went on holiday to France and this almost marked the start of the four of us being an independent small family, without relying on other members of the wider family or friends to help us out when we wanted to do ordinary things like going out for days, going on holiday etc. I say *almost*, as on this trip there were twelve of us; my brother and his family, my cousin, Paul, his family and the four of us. We travelled

JANE COUPES

in convoy by car from Stockport to Poole, Dorset, where we stayed in a Travel Lodge for one night, before catching the early morning ferry from Poole to Cherbourg.

An appropriate 'weather window' was what we had to wait for before we could drive onto the ferry. The conditions were bad that morning, so we had to sit around on the quay for quite a while. The children were restless and couldn't wait to get together on the ferry, so that they could explore and play. Our weather window soon came and we began the military operation that is the cars rolling onto the cross-channel ferry and parking up.

Finally on deck, we sat in a room right at the front of the ferry. They said our weather window had arrived; however, the conditions were still really bad. We had chosen the fast ferry. None of us had ever experienced it before and I'm not sure we would ever choose it again. The waves crashed over the side, people were vomiting in the toilets and sinks, even the staff staggered about everywhere. The others said they felt very unsteady and I did too; however, at that time, even when I walked on terra firma I felt unsteady all the time, so was actually quite adept at getting about the boat.

Staying in three caravans situated together, it was great for the children to wander around the campsite freely. My highlight of our holiday was when we met up with my old work colleague and friend, Jill, and her family, who were holidaying a short drive down the coast.

When they drove to our campsite, we had a huge barbecue complete with 'cheval' meat for Andrew, but we never told him what he was eating! This barbecue was also to celebrate the 50th anniversary of the queen's coronation. I was also a little shocked on this holiday, as even though by now at home I was quite independent at preparing simple meals etc., when

I was in an unfamiliar and small kitchen I suddenly felt quite disabled again, making me feel as though it was a huge step backwards to that time when I was in hospital and so dependent. Although we ate at restaurants every night, it meant Dom had to prepare all the breakfasts and lunches and again, this felt quite alien and very frustrating to me, as before I had been the one in charge of cooking. It was almost as if we had experienced a role reversal within our relationship!

This was our first ever holiday with Daniel and, although it was quite difficult for me, it was also a huge relief and the much needed break for the four of us since our drama had unfolded.

JANE COUPES

A Rush of Blood
to the Head!

The seventh event, or fundamental thing that happened, was one of my favourites and something I had wanted to recreate soon. In fact, after having initial heart problems, my first two questions to Dr Lewis were:

"Can I still make love to my husband and will I be allowed on the big rides at Alton Towers again?"

I was worried about any implications of my heart racing again and what damage this could do. This year, during one of my six-monthly reviews, I actually made him commit to answers.

"Keep everything in moderation, and you should be fine," was his answer to my first question.

To my second, he replied with something along the lines of:

"Well, you may black out completely with the pressure to your brain, but apart from that, you should be okay."

I told Dom that even though I was a little apprehensive,

it was something that I really did want to explore again, as I had always been a bit of a thrill seeker on those big rides.

We decided to have a break during Emily's first February half-term and stay in the Alton Towers Hotel. When you stay in the hotel the guests have exclusive access to a section of the park for either a morning or afternoon, and ours was a morning session in the section that includes the Air and Nemesis rides. The queues were moving so quickly that Dominic was able to go on first while I looked after Emily and Daniel, strapped into his buggy, and then we switched and Dom was able to help me get belted in and help me off the rides afterwards. It was great to feel that exhilaration again and I was a little bit disorientated when I came off, but soon recovered. Another high-flying goal completed!

Six months later I had my next review with Dr Lewis.

"As a doctor, during your career, you always have one patient that you will never ever forget and you're mine!" he said.

This felt like high praise indeed, considering some of the patients he must have seen during his long and varied career.

In contrast, the eighth thing that happened in terms of my recovery during this year was very sad and soul-searching. I found myself in a situation where I had to attend the funeral of one of my close rehab friends in the late summer of that year. It was Julie's funeral, my friend with whom I had spent time in the next room, and basically her malignant brain tumour came back and her condition had deteriorated during that summer, until sadly she died in a nursing home. She had been the same age as me and I was totally devastated, as were my other rehab friends, who also attended the funeral. I remember the cremation well and at the end they played the

JANE COUPES

song by Sting, 'Fields of Gold.' Dom's dad escorted me to the funeral and he could see that we were all devastated.

After this event it was really strange because as a survivor you then feel guilty, and from that moment it was almost as if I decided that I had to make my life better and fuller, and get that full recovery for Julie, Bob, my GP rehab friend whose funeral I had attended in the autumn of 2001, and all the other people stuck in hospitals, who are the true victims of long-term illness. I felt a very strong need to make some positive things happen after a totally negative situation in which I had found myself.

The ninth and final thing that happened during this year was quite vain, but nevertheless, quite a big leap for a woman. I decided that now my way of life had changed and I would be spending lots of time at the gym, it was time to have my hair cut very short. I was in fact struggling to care for it with only one arm functioning properly, so this made washing, drying and styling quite difficult, so I decided it was the right thing to do.

Now I was panicking about going to the hairdressers in my wheelchair. I had ventured there a couple of times at weekends already with Dom, but found it quite stressful. On a weekend visit whilst in hospital I had gone from shoulder length hair to my hair being cut in a short bob - now it was time to go more drastic.

In actual fact, when the boyish impish style was done, I quite liked it and wondered why I hadn't had the courage to do it before when Emily was a baby and time in the shower became shortened.

~

In the spring of 2003, we moved house and area to Marple

Bridge, which was where we had chosen to send our children to school. In fact, the school is St Mary's RC School, the very same one Dom had attended as a boy. This was part of our grand plan for me finally caring for my own children without any additional help, and meant it was time to raise my game.

Our move to Marple Bridge was either brave or stupid on my part, considering I could no longer drive. Marple Bridge is a semi-rural location situated on the edge of the Peak District. Homer Drive is our new address and the second right turn off a hill called Bonington Rise. I'm not sure what the gradient is, but it's pretty steep and I'm sure Chris Bonington would be proud to accomplish it. This move and this hill were to play a huge part in my heart rehabilitation.

I told Nick, my instructor at the gym, about my move to Marple Bridge and that our long-term aim would be that I could walk the children to and from school every day. He knew the area, so we changed my gym programme accordingly and he introduced me to 'pyramids' on the treadmill. This is a programme whereby you push the incline setting up after each minute until you reach your top marker then press down again to your bottom marker and keep repeating, and it is supposed to simulate hill walking. When you are a quarter of the way through the programme you should be on your top marker, halfway through on the bottom etc. I also increased the speed and length of time that I could walk on the treadmill at this time. I was also pleasantly pleased when I learned that I could now blow my nose with my good hand and still continue walking and balancing without holding on to the rails of the treadmill at all. Another minor triumph!

Our house move was also the end of an era for us. I felt like the house in Offerton where we had initially had so many hopes and aspirations had not lived up to those very high expectations. Instead, it could as well have been the house from the film *The Omen*, as it carried lots of demons for me. Although the St John's Wood house had been where as a brand new baby I had brought Daniel home, it was also the house were my health had deteriorated rapidly and I had eventually been spirited away in an ambulance only to return seven months later, a very different person left with severe injuries. The only thing I was sad to leave were our neighbours, Alan, Fiona, Matthew and Mickie, and also our friends, Trevor and Caroline, who lived around the corner.

I was also looking forward to a new start. Marple Bridge was where our future was and still is. This was where we had chosen a fantastic school for Emily and Daniel to attend, and it was definitely the backdrop for the next stage of my rehabilitation.

This move also cast a dark shadow over our family and marked the start of some dark times for us. David Hinds was right when he said the effects and aftermath of a stroke are very difficult to deal with. It started the day after we had moved into Homer Drive, with a petty argument about which box the cornflakes had been packed away in by the removal guys. I was unable to give myself or the children breakfast, as Dom had no idea where our cereals were. He had been the only person around our old house on the previous day when the removal firm had come in to pack up all our worldly goods, so I felt he should know the answer to that simple question. I had been frustrated about not being able to be at home on packing up day anyway. They packed up on a Thursday and this was one of the days I had to complete my programme at the gym. The children were at nursery, so Dom had assured me that everything would be under control.

I felt that I couldn't afford to take time off from my rehabilitation even to move house!

Anyway, on that dreadful day we had a massive row and things got so bad that I ended up scratching Dom on his face. I have no idea what made me launch at him and try to attack him, but I am hugely ashamed to say that I did so. Blokes can be so infuriating sometimes! After living for months in hospital with people who had unacceptable behaviour, I immediately knew that what I had done was wrong and I had hit rock bottom. I guess it must have just been months of anger, frustration and not progressing as quickly as I wanted to, my feelings still masked by the dreaded anti-depressants and also the stress of moving house. Maybe I had bottled it all up until now (or 'internalised' it, which is the term the experts use!). If I had recovered more quickly, I would not have needed to attend the gym and, therefore, would have stayed to watch the removal guys pack the stuff away then this stupid argument would not have happened.

It was a time of extremes thereafter. Our relationship was either really good or really bad to the extent that I would often hurl verbal abuse at Dom - there was no in-between. For years we had lived on a calm plane and it was hard to know whether we would have experienced these testing times anyway in our marriage, or if it was the extra extreme pressure under which we had been put. I felt it was definitely the latter.

Now there were lots of slammed doors, lots of times when I walked out of the house to cool off on a short walk. All the time I felt bad in case Emily and Daniel were to pick up on what was happening. I told Dom that we were no longer compatible, and called him lots of nasty names. As the swear words rolled off my tongue with ease, I was horrified when I heard the foul words come out. Every time I went on a rant, he ignored me and remained very calm. At the time I thought he was weak to stay with me and not retaliate, and I truly believe that had our original relationship not been based on great friendship, we would not still be together now. I guess all my single-mindedness towards my recovery had to come at a price and challenge my relationships with others!

Anyone who knows me will know that I have always had a stroppy side, but I had never been physical since play-fighting with my brother, Andrew, when we were children. I guess the pressure of our situation just made me crack. How awful for Dom to go in to work and tell white lies saying that he had been gardening and some bushes had scratched his face!

In contrast, after my monthly rant it was great to do all the making up and, although I knew we had serious problems, I also felt that we had actually coped quite well with the extreme pressure under which our marriage had been put. We had never had a tumultuous relationship before, so this really was new and unknown territory for us. We were tested to the limit, but both still wanted it to work out, so that we could draw a line under this awful chapter in our relationship and be a happy family again. Although the 'divorce' word was mentioned on numerous occasions, neither of us really wanted to go down that route and, as we still love each other heaps and were still experiencing some good times (although now few and far between!), decided to soldier on.

I can only reiterate that I immediately knew that my behaviour was unacceptable, whatever the reason, so started to make enquiries about receiving some counselling, so that I could move on from this horrible place. Dom decided that he didn't want to join me in this pursuit, as he felt that lots of our joint problems were mostly the effects of the psychological changes in my unique situation. I was slightly disappointed with his decision and felt we would both have benefited from counselling together.

At that time I felt totally undermined in every aspect of our children's well-being. I had extremely high standards before my stroke and now started to feel that some of them had been compromised slightly. I had no choice but to accept any extra help that was on offer, but I felt that it was time to start making myself heard again. Unfortunately, as there were so many strong emotions tied into my children and their care, my words often came out as criticism or sounded aggressive. What can I say? Like any mother, I just wanted the best for my children and, to this day, I am still the one who knows all their little quirks and traits better than anyone else. Dominic and I started to unintentionally undermine each other's decisions and I felt that the whole dynamic of our family had been changed.

~

In 2003 I was referred to a counsellor at Stepping Hill Hospital. I remember the sessions quite well. During my first one the counsellor just asked me to talk. She knew I had been referred after having a stroke.

"I find it really difficult to talk about," were my first words.

I then proceeded to talk non-stop, whilst sobbing uncontrollably for an entire hour, until my first session was over!

I continued to see her over a period of ten weeks and just off-loaded lots of stresses and strains. She also gave me some techniques to enable me to deal with the psychological effects of my stroke, and these I took on board and still use on my less frequent 'off' days. At some point during our sessions, she helped me to stop thinking of myself as a victim and started

JANE COUPES

to give me a very different outlook on life once that I had accepted the fact that I am now a survivor and proud of it!

We had one misunderstanding during our sessions, which really upset me. She said that I needed to 'accept it and move on.' I misunderstood her and took that to mean that I should just give up and accept living a life where people needed to help me with everyday tasks like cutting up food, fastening my bra etc. I felt that if I had taken this advice earlier in my illness, I would still have been totally reliant on my wheelchair.

In the next session, however, I told her how upset I had been and she clarified what she had meant, which was that I had to accept that my stroke was now part of my life and that at some point when I have stopped progressing, I was going to be left with physical injuries, so would just need to start a new life from that point.

Accepting it felt as though it was totally against my strategy, which was to fight it head on, put lots of effort into my physiotherapy sessions and get the best recovery possible, so that I would no longer require help from other parties. After that session I was so upset that when I went to pick Emily up from school I could not stop crying. However, it was yet another issue I had to deal with, so I stood and waited for Emily in the playground, but away from my friends or anyone who might pick up on my sadness, or ask why I was upset.

Nice try, but my friend, Colette, soon realised that something was wrong. She was my old school friend also from Harrytown, in fact, the very same class in which Dom and I had been. She had been unable to face visiting me in hospital and seeing me so poorly; however, soon after my discharge she called around to our house in Offerton with a huge bunch of flowers. She had just moved to Marple Bridge at that time and I told her we had plans to follow her. She started to call around on a regular basis thereafter.

Now our children both attend the same school and our daughters, who are in the same class, are very friendly and our boys also love getting together, despite the small age gap of exactly one year to the day, yes, they share the same birthday, 24th February. Colette then turned out to be one of my closest and hugest supports thereafter.

I told most of my close friends that I was receiving counselling and we joked about the lady whom I was seeing when I described her.

"Well, she looks like she wears men's clothes sometimes, along with red shoes, and she holidays in Borneo," I said.

"It sounds like she needs counselling herself," we joked.

In truth, the sessions were very helpful to me and when they finished I felt better equipped to deal with difficult or stressful situations. She also explained that I had to 'normalise' situations. Often I felt completely stressed out and had attributed those symptoms to my stroke, rather than that my life was getting busier as I got better, and I was now sometimes just a stressed-out mother of two now unable to drive, but still had all the tasks and running around to complete just like any other parent!

Meanwhile, Emily had started in reception class at St Mary's School and was doing well. She had a huge learning curve ahead of her and I also had a steep learning curve too, but mine was more physical. I now needed to and thoroughly enjoyed walking Emily to and from school every day, whilst also conserving enough energy to look after her when we returned, and also make preparations for our evening meal when Dominic and Daniel returned from work/ nursery. I soon had everything geared up, so that when Dom and Daniel returned we could have our meal then get the children bathed and ready for bed. Often I was so shattered (after all my hill walking) that I would go to bed as soon as Emily and Daniel did, even if it was only seven or eight o'clock at night! Once we were all tucked up in bed, this became the time when Dom started to go running in the evenings on a frequent basis. Now we rarely had that time when it was just the two of us and we could chat or watch television together. I really did miss that time, but was just so tired that I couldn't wait to get to bed in the evenings.

Taking Emily down to school was hard work for me to begin with. I was worried about running late in the mornings, as I could no longer run to get Emily down to school at the last minute. I had special dispensation so that if Dom had to go in to work early or was away on business, Emily was able to go to school without her top button on her blouse fastened. These were too stiff for me to tackle and she was unable to do them at only four! Emily's teacher at the school was a joy. She was also the deputy head at the school at that time and I could see that she worked really hard. She was always there to supervise the playground from 8.30 a.m., she could play the guitar and lead in songs during assembly. She seemed to stay late lots and she even represented the staff at the PTA meetings, which I started to attend when I had enough energy to stay up late. The meetings usually finished between 9 p.m. and 10 p.m., but this was now considered late for me, especially as they tended to hold them on Wednesday evenings and the next day was religiously gym day for me, when I needed to be able to fully concentrate on my programme.

When I went down to school I found it difficult to negotiate the steps down to the playground, as this was the first time I had done any sort of steps without handrails. I just got on with it as Mike, my physiotherapist whilst in hospital, had once said that I needed to get used to some obstacles in the real world, as it would do me good to stress my brain out from time to time.

I also found the noise level difficult to cope with and the fact that there were children running around in all directions. Previously that had been one of the worst scenarios for my brain to deal with, and it was a while before I could hold a conversation with another parent and still keep track of where Emily had gone in the playground.

Emily loved school from the start (she was almost born to go to school!) and she took all the new challenges in her stride. She would often continue to play classrooms at home when she returned from school and sometimes she would pretend to call the register and even copy out her many 'Pupil of the Week' certificates and award them to her dolls and teddies! She even picked up small traits from her teacher and she started tucking her hair behind her ear in exactly the same way that I had seen her teacher do from time to time!

JANE COUPES

Living the Dream!

Emily starting school was also great for me, as I met lots of other parents in and around the playground. St Mary's is a very close-knit Catholic school family and you would struggle to find a friendlier group of parents anywhere. I have experienced very little negative playground gossip in the whole time Emily has been at St Mary's and it was in fact a huge positive for me to have a community around me and at last people to say, 'Good morning' or 'How are you?' to as I walked amongst them. I can honestly say that I have made many good friends, some whom I knew before and some whom I have met at a later date. Quite a few of the other parents in Emily's class were in fact people from our year group at Harrytown, so it can be like a school reunion. Parents would offer me a lift back up the hill, but most of the time I politely declined unless it was absolutely pouring with rain or snowing. I always thanked them anyway, but also had to stay true to my heart rehabilitation and make sure I completed a vigorous, but very slow, walk every day!

Marple Bridge is very hilly and is the kind of place that if you are not going up a hill, you are going down one! My hike up the hill was invigorating and obviously got my heart rate going, as when I returned home in the mornings I felt great and then would begin a cleaning frenzy. By the afternoon I was completely shattered, and for the first time I felt that my heart condition and stroke symptoms were almost competing head on!

St Mary's children are the best - great personalities, the most attractive group of children in smart uniforms you could ever wish to meet (none with straight hair and curly teeth!) - and when I saw them in the playground I started to test myself on calling them by their individual names, which I picked up during assembly times. Another test for my grey matter!

As I now had a little more time during the school day, it was the time when two key things happened. I was granted ill health retirement from my previous job at Barclays, which led to me investing a large portion of my leaving package and then spending the residual on private physiotherapy at home.

My retirement was granted speedily without the usual necessity of me having to visit the bank's doctor in London. They just wrote to my cardiologist and neurological consultants, and I guess their written reports indicated that it was unlikely that I would work again in my previous capacity, if at all, with the degree of injuries I had sustained.

I had very mixed feelings about this decision. At the time I was still so poorly that it just seemed a bit of a result that Barclays were in effect paying me (albeit a small monthly pension plus reasonable lump sum) to stay at home and look after my children, especially when there was so much restructuring going on within the company that my old job may have disappeared anyway. There was also the realisation that ill health retirement is quite a final decision, meaning that my career was over and yet again another of my life choices had been taken away. I had always intended to go back to work part-time after having Daniel, so although I made the most of the time to look after my young family at last, there were also sad feelings too.

~

Dominic and I did some research on the Internet to find a neurological physiotherapist in our area. Neurological physiotherapy is different to other types of physiotherapy, and below is a brief explanation why.

Neurophysiotherapy is a rehabilitation approach, where the physiotherapist communicates with the central nervous system and peripheral nervous system (the brain and the body).

Communicating with the nervous system enables us to learn and thus develop usable functions like:

- walking;
- lifting a cup to your mouth;
- lifting your arm in an efficient pattern of movement.

Approaching treatment from a neurological perspective, i.e. talking to the nervous system, is a method of treatment in any condition or disease that causes alterations in movement patterns; for example, stroke, multiple sclerosis, stiff knee.

The treatment concept requires a physical 'hands on' approach, where the therapist is communicating with the nervous system and muscular system. The therapist will be aiming to make immediate local changes to muscle tone (activity), and the circulation, where hands are in contact, but also more general changes to posture and muscle activity via the communication with the nervous system. The ultimate aim is to enable the patient to have a better, more efficient quality of movement.

As neurological physiotherapists are so specialised and, therefore, thin on the ground, it took us a while to find a suitable one. After speaking to Dr Downton, she recommended a small team of physiotherapists working in the Stockport area, so I rang the contact number and was put in touch with my current physiotherapist, Tina. I immediately got on with her and we set to work improving my posture and walking. She is very 'hands on' and, although we chat whilst working, she never stops manipulating/working my muscles for our whole hour session. Tina has a very bubbly personality and is a real tonic to have visiting your home. She is only tiny, but she works me hard and pummels me, so that when she leaves I feel like I have fought ten rounds with Mike Tyson! Her techniques are very progressive and she is always attending courses and trying out new ones on me!

The sessions are costly, but I get a good feeling that my leaving package (in essence a pay off for being robbed of my career and the progression that I was never able to optimise due to ill health) is being spent wisely on my recovery. At this time Tina also set me a realistic programme of exercises that I do every day religiously when the children are in school, and this means that I can now stretch shortened muscles and keep 'on top of my injuries' by myself.

If I was forced to have a bone of contention with Tina it would be that one of my exercises has caused me to have

JANE COUPES

stretch marks on my left calf muscle. This exercise is intended to stretch that particular set of muscles and improve my walking. I have obviously got it off to a tee as I must stretch them so well that there is a permanent marker there to show it! After carrying two babies and luckily getting away without having one single stretch mark on my body, this was not good news.

~

For a time spending my lump sum was bearable and, although it felt unfair that I should have to pay for such a service myself, as a coping mechanism I had to. I just buried my head in the sand for a while and pretended it was okay.

By pure chance my dad came into contact with someone who had worked for Stockport Primary Care Trust and he suggested that we should try to get some funding towards my physiotherapy treatment, as really they still had a duty of care to me. Again we found ourselves in a situation where we had to fight for funding, which at first was not forthcoming. This was increasingly disheartening and sometimes when I was involved with typing letters and worrying about the possible outcome, I felt it took the focus off my recovery and knocked some of my impetus to battle on.

~

2004 was a very important year for Daniel and I, as this was when he started nursery at St Mary's and was the first time we had been at home together, just the two of us, for any proper length of time.

I had already decided to relish and totally cherish our time, and put any chores on hold for when I had dropped him off at nursery. To enable this to happen, we decided that the only feasible way I could cope with Daniel (who is a very physical and boisterous little boy!) was to get permission for him to attend St Mary's Nursery for three mornings a week (instead of the standard five sessions of nursery provision that is the norm) and still continue with his two full days at Happy Day Nursery, so I could still get to the gym and have that all important rest day. We had to get permission to do this from the head teacher at the school. She was very obliging in our unique circumstances and, consequently, we had a whole magical year of mornings when we just played, learned the alphabet, read books and sometimes walked into the village together, always calling at the post office for a treat for Daniel and Emily.

During this year I continued with my physiotherapy. The only difference was that Daniel sometimes disrupted our sessions when Tina, my physiotherapist, called, and I could no longer lie on the floor to do my daily exercises when he was around, as he thought I wanted to wrestle him!

We really did gel during this time and Daniel was occasionally able to sometimes assist me with things that I was unable to do. He would sometimes carry the washing basket up and down the stairs for me, and one snowy day we showed great teamwork, as together we were able to almost tie a knot in the laces of Mummy's winter boots, so that we could venture out (holding each other up!) and post a birthday card, making spectacular tracks in the snow!

I particularly remember our first time that we walked into the village together. Dom was completely paranoid about us going out together, as Daniel was only three and totally unwilling to hold my hand. I convinced Daniel that if he wanted to do nice things then we had to be extra careful. We had to

JANE COUPES

drum into him that 'Mummy cannot chase you if you run off because Mummy has a poorly arm and leg.' It eventually sunk in and we got to a point where he was good at holding my hand for the entire journey to nursery. However, he didn't always do it on the way home, as now big sister, Emily, was around and it was quite good fun to chase her and deviate off the pavement onto the grass verges.

On our first adventure we called at the doctor's to collect my repeat prescription for my myriad of drugs, and I also needed to order some flowers. We called at the chemist to collect my medication and Daniel climbed onto a low wooden shelf and nearly became part of the window display. We went down the stone stairs into the florist's cellar.

"How did these flowers grow down here?" he asked the lady. "Are we in a cave? Are there any bears in here?"

It was wonderful for me to know that my son had become a naturally inquisitive and mischievous little boy, just like any other three year old. For the very first time since he was born, I felt like we had a natural mother-son relationship.

Before this time I had found it strange that when I had taken Emily down to school, none of the other mums (whom I knew were aware that I also had Daniel) ever asked me where he was. I felt as though I was an unfit mother whose child was in nursery when I wasn't presently working. When I eventually started to take them both down together, it was strange to me that no one commented on how good it was that he was now in tow all the time. I sometimes felt he was like 'the invisible child' in the playground. Why couldn't everyone else see that it was indeed a small miracle that we were together in this way at last?

Also at this time, I took over responsibility for reading Daniel and Emily's bedtime story again. Their favourite books at that time were the *Percy the Park Keeper* series of books by Nick Butterworth. I totally bought into this non-physical activity with Daniel, and did lots of silly character voices and actions to get him interested again. They both loved Mummy's story time so much that they started to argue over whether Mummy or Daddy read their individual story. This was a rewarding feeling after years of me almost racing the children to bed as I was so severely fatigued! At this time, Dom and I made an unintentional initial arrangement that he would do physical stuff with them and I would do the reading/writing stuff.

~

2005 was also a catalyst year in terms of Daniel's development, for this was the year when it was his turn to follow his big sister, Emily, and start in reception class at St Mary's School. Like many schools, they do a staggered intake to ensure that the children settle well, so his very first day in reception class was an afternoon session only and at first it just felt like the old routine of nursery.

As I helped Daniel to put on his uniform, I realised that it was in fact another turning point and a time of great significance for us. We had been on such a long journey to get to a stage where I could hold his hand and walk him to school that my emotions were riding high. We walked down the hill and Daniel was particularly interested in some workmen who were resurfacing the pavement, totally taking his big day in his stride. We had already been on a special trip to meet his new teachers and he had impressed us by confidently bounding into the classroom by himself, way ahead of us.

Using the back door at the school, which is the entrance to the reception classroom, I chatted to a few other parents as

JANE COUPES

I walked away in slightly pensive and choked mood. Quite a few of the other mums were also tearful as their babies were starting school for the first time. Daniel was my youngest and now to be my last baby, and this was behind my quiet reflection too, but also our poignant and very long journey and all that we had achieved together was very much on my mind. Who could have thought when I was so poorly in hospital that I would ever have been well enough to walk 'hand in hand' with my son on his first day at school? Totally preoccupied as I walked home, I tramped straight across where the workmen had just put tarmac down on the pavement and left a couple of my trainer footprints! I apologised to the guys profusely and headed home to ring Dom in a tearful mist about Daniel's huge milestone and our next hugely significant completed goal.

I feel like I fully embraced this time with the children and saw the importance of being able to walk them to and from school every day. I felt I was there by default, as I knew that without my stroke I would have returned to work by now and they would have had to go to breakfast and after-school club, and maybe sacrifice some of the many activities in which they are lucky enough to take part. We also had lots of friends over for tea and I went down to every event that went on at school, being fortunate enough not to have to take time off and cut short what would have been my working day in Manchester to do so!

Marathon Man

Since the early days of Dom's running, he had now started competing in road races dotted around the country. I particularly recall one December morning when I took Emily as a toddler in (and out of!) her buggy to watch Dom run the 'Stockport 10' race. Wrapped up in my huge brown chenille woolly jumper, we camped out in Woodbank Park, so we could watch the start and finish, and actually have refreshments and a seat, as by this time I was now also pregnant with Daniel. I remember Dom being overwhelmingly enthusiastic.

"Do you think you'll join me in a race when you've had the baby?" he asked.

For the first time ever since going to watch lots of events, I could understand how runners catch that bug; however, there was only ever a miniscule chance of me ever running with Dom. We really had no idea of how our lives were about to change. Since that time a lot has happened and we have both experienced progression in our fitness levels, for totally different reasons.

JANE COUPES

Now tension was rising. Finally, after months of training and hard work for Dom, and also four long months, with no weekends off for me looking after the kids while he did so, the big weekend arrived. Dom had big plans to run the London Marathon (his first ever one!) on Sunday, 17th April, 2005. It was also Emily's sixth birthday weekend and we were very excited. I was also a little nervous. I worried that Dom's training would not pay off and he would hit the infamous 'wall.'

As a mum I felt under pressure and was also concerned that Emily's birthday would not be fantastic. We had planned to have a party with all her school friends a couple of weeks later, but I wanted it to be special for her and was concerned that all the emphasis would be on Dom and not her.

On the Friday, with lots of planning to do, I set about getting clothes out for us to take at the weekend. Emily was being presented with a Head Teacher's Award in assembly that day, so my dad rang to confirm that he was able to come up and watch her receive it. The phone rang.

"Hi, Jane, how are you?"

"Not bad," I replied.

"What does *not bad* mean?"

I then broke down in tears.

"It means not good."

My hormones were flying everywhere and I was a wreck. I told my dad about my fears.

"You will have a great weekend and so will Emily," he said. "Don't worry."

After my tears I calmed down and felt a big release. I was in fact going to really enjoy the weekend. It had been a long time coming before we could actually realise this dream of Dom's. Four years on from my stroke and we were embarking on a big adventure, going to London, Dom running the marathon and hopefully raising lots of money for our charity, Different Strokes, which is for younger stroke survivors, like myself. We had spent weeks asking people to sponsor Dom, we had sent emails to all our friends, family and acquaintances and Dom had even set up a website where people could sponsor him online.

Dom's colleague from work, Mark, was also running with him and supporting an autism charity, and I was looking forward to comparing notes with his wife as to how it had been a hard onslaught to get them to this big event with all the preparations of training, extra healthy meals etc. Dom's mum and dad were also coming with us to watch and to help me look after the children while Dom did vital preparation before the race.

Emily and Daniel were really excited, as we had decided to make a real weekend of it and fly down, and we had also booked for us to go on the London Eye on the Saturday evening of Emily's birthday. We had already been on the eye when I was twelve weeks pregnant with Daniel and we went down to London for a few days sightseeing. I enjoyed telling the kids that they had both already technically been on the eye, but this time they would be able to appreciate it better.

After a bit of a dash on the Saturday morning, our taxi arrived at 8 a.m. No lie-in again for us this weekend and we set off to pick up Margaret and Vincent, and then onwards to the airport. The children were so excited at being in the airport and they sat and played games while we waited for our flight to be announced. Once we got to Heathrow Airport, we caught the Heathrow Express to Paddington Station. Daniel was excited about going on so many different methods of transport and we had to talk about them all. I was pleased that I was still fairly familiar with London from a

JANE COUPES

trip that Dom and I had taken the previous November for our wedding anniversary.

We arrived at the hotel, which was really plush and swanky. I began to wonder if the children would be made to feel welcome in such a nice hotel. We went to check out our rooms and they were equally as sumptuous, although Mark and Louise were a little disappointed that their room was on the small side. Emily and Daniel would sleep on a sofa bed in Margaret and Vincent's room. This meant that Dom would be guaranteed a good night's sleep, without any little intruders! I was a little disappointed with our bathroom, only because there was no walk-in shower. By then I could use a shower by stepping over the bath, but since my stroke it just hadn't felt as safe to do it without Dom being there. I knew he would have to be off early in the morning to get to the start of the race, so I was a little concerned.

After inspecting our rooms, we walked along the Embankment and over the river. It was vital that we checked out some Italian restaurants for later that evening before we were booked on the London Eye. It had to be pasta of course, so that the boys could do some carbo-loading! Being marathon weekend, London was especially busy and I found it quite difficult to keep up the pace whilst walking in the crowds. I had done it before since my stroke, but that didn't mean I had to like it!

Dom and Mark had to cross London, as they had to register their numbers for the race the following day. Louise went off to an exhibition that she wanted to see, so Margaret, Vincent and I decided how best to entertain the children. We had all agreed to meet back at the hotel at five-ish, so that we could reconvene and head over to the chosen and pre-booked pasta restaurant.

Hamleys toy store and a ride on an open-top red London bus were decided on, after a lot of thought. We boarded the cheapest bus service and started to cruise along, taking in some of the sights in London, including Big Ben, which had featured on an episode of *Doctor Who* the previous week! The bus seemed to take a long time, and as the weather wasn't brilliant it was actually quite chilly on the top of the bus and the children were cold!

We then took the children to Hamleys toy store, which we explored, then stopped for refreshments where Emily and Daniel were both fascinated by a train set that ran on a track around the edge of the café.

On the big day we awoke early and I felt as though I was sitting a vital exam that day. I had huge butterflies in my tummy for Dom. He was very cool, calm and collected, but just wanted to get on with his preparation before the race. He was able to wait after all while I showered before he went out. He had already been down to breakfast for some porridge with Mark. At that time I was reading Paula Radcliffe's autobiography and I said to Dom that maybe he should drink some green tea like Paula does before a marathon. He said that he couldn't try anything new before his race, as it would be a disaster.

Having already chosen a good spot to watch the race the day before, we were hoping to watch it from around the 25-mile marker, so we could spur Dom on for that last mile. We decided to have a leisurely breakfast and go and take our positions at just after 11 a.m., around the time (according to *Runners World* magazine) that Paula Radcliffe and the elite women would run past! I have heard it said before that the night before the marathon, London is transformed into a very different city. When we eventually got outside, we found this

JANE COUPES

was the case, as the road had been cordoned off and we could not get to the spot we had chosen the previous day. We just decided to wait as close to that spot as we could physically get with all the crowds, so that Dom would know roughly where to look for us. We eventually found a spot that would do.

The crowd was a few deep away from the barriers and we took up our positions and hoped that some people would get fed up and go, so we could get closer. Just then there was a buzz in the crowd and we saw some of the elite runners, including Paula Radcliffe, go past exactly on time (this was even with a famous pit stop!). We waited an age and then runners started to come in small groups. Since Dom had taken up running and I had taken up being a spectator, I had decided that it is actually quite a hard job to do. It is really hard to pick out your person in a crowd, especially when the runners come past at a pace, and sometimes their movement makes it seem as though the road is moving and you can feel a little dizzy!

We stood clapping and cheering for hours, and then our patience started to pay off. Some of the crowd started to move away (they had already seem their family member/friend come past, or just got fed up), so the children squirmed their way right to the front next to the barrier. Soon a few more people left for a smoke and we were all able to move right next to the barrier. This was around about the two-hour mark. We still had a very long wait and my back was already aching, as I was unused to standing for such a long time. I had already booked for my physiotherapist to come to the house the following day and I commented, saying she would be cross with me for putting my body through my own personal marathon of standing for hours on end. However, there was no way I was moving anywhere until I saw Dom, and made sure he was safe and well and had not been injured or had hit the infamous 'wall'!

Around the four-hour time, we were excited and concerned. He was aiming for less than four hours and had put in all the required training, so we were excited knowing that he would soon run past. However, there was still some concern that he wasn't here just yet.

By this time, Dom's cousin and her family had joined us (they lived in Reading and had caught the train to London for the day to cheer him on), so Maria's husband took their children, Sean and Niamh, and also Emily and Daniel to a nearby park to give them a run. They were still within earshot and would be able to dash over to see Daddy.

I cannot remember the number of times someone said, 'Here he is' and it was a false alarm. Another hard factor is that even though you think your person has chosen a bright individual top or costume, it is really hard to pick them out and in actual fact in the crowds it seemed that everyone was wearing the same royal blue running top as Dom! Eventually we saw him and Vincent took some video footage of him running past. Dominic stopped briefly, gave myself, Emily and Daniel a big kiss and carried on with a determined look on his face. I could tell he was struggling, but us standing right at the end had obviously paid off and spurred him on to the finishing line.

The following week I called in to see Margaret at work and she was telling her colleagues about him running past us.

"He stopped and gave all his treasures a kiss, but I didn't get one."

I quickly came back to her.

"Well, it was a very sweaty kiss, so you didn't miss much!"

JANE COUPES

Now much improved, walking better, having built my stamina up to a level where I could mostly do what I wanted to, it was now just over a year and a half later in November 2006 and our next stop was New York City, the Big Apple. Dom was trying to better his last marathon time and crack that four-hour target, and this time he was raising money for St Mary's School PTA, which by now we are involved in by having supporting roles.

This trip was also a celebration of a special wedding anniversary for us.

"Jane, let's go to New York to celebrate our tenth wedding anniversary," Dom had said. Later he suddenly dropped into the conversation, "By the way, while we are there I will also be running the marathon!"

My first impressions of New York were steam rising from the pavements, NYPD cops smoking on street corners, yellow New York cabs bumper to bumper on the streets and lots of high-rise buildings, forming a dramatic skyline. As I craned my neck to look out of the taxi window, I couldn't even see the top of some of the buildings. After being in the city a few days, you soon learn that there are two key things that make New York work as a city; diversity and density. People of all races live literally on top of one another and it just works.

We were complete tourists on this trip and took in The Empire State Building, Grand Central Station, where we had a leisurely lunch and watched the New Yorkers go by, The Rockefeller Center and the Statue of Liberty (where we climbed the 156 steps to the observation deck, rather than taking the lift - because I can!). We also explored Times Square where our hotel was situated and we had a drink in the revolving bar on top of the hotel and were charged for 'the rocks' that accompanied my Baileys! We took a romantic horse-drawn carriage ride through Central Park and familiarised ourselves with the layout, especially the finish in time for race day, which was on the following day.

Very soon race day arrived and the 37th ING New York City Marathon was totally hyped up to be a huge event in America. I had initial doubts about what I would do on race day in New York by myself, but although I didn't fully know my bearings and got confused with the streets and avenues, I did feel quite safe and at ease walking slowly around the city.

Dom left at 5.30 a.m., so I went back to bed for a while after I had wished him luck and saw he was focused and ready to go. Stirring an hour or so later, I rang Emily and Daniel back in the UK and then took a shower and turned the television on to watch the race build-up and the official starts. I had already pre-ordered my room service breakfast, so sat and ate that whilst listening to the build-up and looking out to see if I could get a glimpse of Dom at a place called Fort Wadsworth, where the 37,000 runners were sitting in the dusky sunrise waiting to begin their marathon.

I stood on the corner of Central Park and Columbus Circle, near the famous Trump building for four and a half hours in the freezing cold and still somehow missed Dom run past me. I was receiving text messages from Dom's dad back home as to his progress around the course. This was being relayed to Vincent by email from the New York City Marathon website, which sends emails to your chosen people when they pass over mats around the course every ten kilometres, by way of a chip that Dom was wearing in his running shoe. Four hours, two minutes and 59 seconds was his official time on this occasion. He had knocked a substantial fifteen minutes off his previous marathon time, but still hadn't smashed his own very high target of four hours or less!

Lost amidst the 37,000 runners, their families and supporters near the finish, I panicked and worried about Dom. I just wanted to be reunited with him again after his race. Unsteady, emotional, very lost and very fatigued, I fought my way through the masses and headed to our pre-arranged meeting place, quite near the Dakota Building on 57th Street, which is the place where John Lennon was shot and where we had visited 'Strawberry Fields' the day before to pay homage. I had spent the entire nine hours since Dom had left in New York alone, (except when I met a lovely lady called Cindy, who was staying in our hotel and also watching her husband run his first ever marathon), and felt proud, but just wanted to share it with Dom, along with a celebratory kiss for his phenomenal achievement!

〜

After marathon day we fitted in some shopping at Macy's for gifts, the Broadway show, *Chicago* and also went to visit the Ground Zero site. This was a very emotional trip for us as I am sure that it is for all the visitors to the site. However, I felt that it had been quite a journey for me to be able to go and see for myself some of the positive things that are taking place, especially when I had watched the events of 11th September, 2001, from my hospital bed, barely able to walk after my stroke.

We looked at the exhibits in the museum section, fought back the tears as we wandered through the gallery of photographs of the people who lost their lives on that fateful day and read the letters from family members. As we walked away we were choked in sorrow, in complete silence, but as we walked back to the hotel we were still *hand in hand*.

Prologue

Complete closure is what I'm seeking from this book. It's all here in black and white should I ever want to dwell on it. If Emily and Daniel want to read it when they are old enough and well equipped to understand what happened and why things were so tough for Mummy and Daddy when they were little, I will allow them to do so.

I think I have now learned that you just do not know what is in store for you. I still want to achieve the best recovery I can, but medical staff will never make assumptions or give any commitment, which I find very frustrating. I sometimes feel that I have had a privileged insight into the world of disabled people. Their world can be a very lonely and intimidating place when you are not fully *compos mentis* and it is one of which I do not want to be a permanent part. However, on my journey I have met many brave and courageous people.

Who knows what is just around the corner for any of us?

If you are reading this and thinking things like that just don't happen to me, I will warn you that I used to think in exactly the same way. Head injuries and strokes happened to other people. However, I have learned the difficult way that they could happen to you or one of your family members and plunge your world into turmoil.

I sometimes think that when I say that I spent six months in rehab, it makes me sound quite rock n' roll. However, the reality is that it was a traumatic and scary time for me, when really I should have been at home with my family, attending post-natal groups and doing typical new mum things.

I'm eight years on now; I have been left with significant injuries to my left arm and am still having good days and bad days, although the bad days are far less frequent nowadays. Occasionally if strangers look twice at me, I get all defensive. A part of me wants to say to them, 'Do you know what has happened to me?' and, 'Do you know how brave I am?.' I hope that with time I will just learn to ignore them, as at the end of the day all the people who care about me and who I care about back have accepted me the way I am. Other times I get this euphoric feeling that I am special. I am a born fighter and have cheated death and survived an experience that would have shattered others.

In addition, I sometimes feel that people who have not had a serious illness just don't understand life, and seem fairly negative. They moan and complain about trivial things and don't count their blessings. I am pretty sure I used to do the same, but now I know something they don't. I have learned the value of health, friends and family the hard way and hope that I have now learned my lesson!

I am desperate to try and live a more relaxed life, but it is very hard with two children. I keep saying that if I am ever lucky enough to be in a position to drive again, I will never complain about traffic jams. I will no longer say that I am tired, because now I know what it is like to experience real

JANE COUPES

fatigue. I actually bet I will in due course, but I can still hold out hope that I will not slip back into those ways.

I have recently celebrated my 40th birthday and am really looking forward to making this stage of my life a new chapter. My thirties have been dominated by childbearing (the good bit) and ill health (not so good!). I feel that hopefully it can only get better for me. I have already experienced what old age is like, as I have had plenty of the trappings and symptoms; however, I think I have demonstrated that you can experience those things and still strive to be positive.

I hope my experience will make me a better person in the course of time, because I did and still do experience phases when I turn into Mrs Angry. There is nothing like a life-threatening illness to put things into perspective.

I sometimes think that the scarring that has occurred on my brain can in no way match the scarring of the fact that I did not spend my son's first few crucial months in a more conventional way, i.e. at home.

A huge part of this book is that I want to thank all those around me who have in any small or large way aided my recovery (they know who they are!) and also for me to give myself a little pat on the back (most unheard of!) and say, 'the girl done good!', and she's not finished yet!

Perseverance is my message to all stroke victims, but the hardest thing to put into practice!

~